INTERNATIONAL TOURISM: WORLD GEOGRAPHY AND DEVELOPMENTAL PERSPECTIVES

Babu P. George, PhD
Pondicherry University, India

&

Alexandru Nedelea, PhD
Univ."Stefan cel Mare", Romania

ABHIJEET PUBLICATIONS

DELHI 110094

ABHIJEET PUBLICATIONS
2/46 Tukhmeerpur Extension
Delhi 110094
Phone: 011-22960492, 65698474
e-mail: abhijeet_singh@vsnl.net
abhijeetpublication@gmail.com

INTERNATIONAL TOURISM: WORLD GEOGRAPHY AND DEVELOPMENTAL PERSPECTIVES

First Published 2007

ISBN 978-81-89886-18-5
Price: Rs. 480/- (INR)

PRINTED IN INDIA

Published by J.K. Singh for Abhijeet Publications, Delhi 110094, Lasertypeset by Rajesh Data Services, New Delhi and Printed at Himanshu Printers, Delhi.

Preface

International Tourism: World Geography and Developmental Perspectives has been framed as a supplementary text book and hence cannot be claimed as an important addition to the extant body of tourism literature. This does not, however, mean that the present volume is totally worthless. On the contrary, its merit lies in successfully sorting out the disparate elements of literature shattered here and there, both in the age-old libraries and in the World Wide Web. This is definitely not done in a mechanical way: the authors' self can be seen peeped out of the analysis that often appears as naturally woven together with the borrowed content.

Let me provide an abstract of each chapter included:

The first chapter, titled *International Tourism: Historical Perspectives,* discusses the historical development of tourism. History helps to develop judgment in worldly affairs. This is because the tendency of things shows an amazing uniformity within any given civilization, or, sometimes even across civilizations. In addition, history of tourism provides us with a number of instructive examples to follow and not to follow. A study of the history of tourism, for good or bad, supports common cultural understanding and dialogue, too. The chapter stresses the beginnings and the growth of mass tourism. Mass tourism is one of the most studied tourism phenomena and it truly deserves a very detailed treatment, which remains unmet in the present volume, largely due to the space constraint. A subsection is devoted to the historical practice of tourism in India. This was felt necessary not so much because the Indian example is unique but because the expected readership for the present volume is largely from India.

The chapter titled *International Tourism: Trends* presents the forces that are influential in drawing the future trajectory of tourism. Trends, though are of the future, are seen from the present. Hence, there is an inevitable proneness for miscalculation. The technological trends are the ones most discussed in the academia and in the industry circles. There exists a great deal of unanimity in the prediction that technology has the potential to revolutionize the travel trade, but not a fraction of the same when it comes to answering how. This chapter, in addition, examines how September 11 has influenced tourism. Everyone who discounted it as merely the fall of two concrete structures had to repent. Another important topic discussed in this chapter is on sustainability. While sustainability has become a marketing plank, the vital issue is 'whose sustainability and for whom?'

The chapter titled *International Tourism: Contemporary Issues* aims to present certain key debates that occur between the past and the future discussed in the previous two chapters. It explores the theory and practice of tourism development, offering alternative approaches to policy issues and extending research into newly developing tourist destinations. Issues discussed include terrorism, flesh trade, gender, globalization, and so on. While there is no dearth of topics, we had to restrict to a few key ones.

The chapter titled *World Geography: Concepts* discusses the concepts of geography in a manner that is important for tourism. Tourism is a place phenomenon and hence geography has always been an important contributory discipline in its academic maturity. The subtopics discussed are: The Five Themes of Geography; Important Geographical Regions; IATA Regions; Important Tourism Destinations of India; and, India: Climate and Seasons. This chapter gives a basic geographic overview of the world and each major geographic region, providing insights about the geographic character of specific regions to show how it establishes a setting for tourism.

The chapter titled *World Geography: Applications* moves closer to the world of practice in that it gives an application orientation to the concepts studied. The subtopics discussed include: Maps and Cartography; Geographical Information System; Wilderness Tourism; Natural Parks; Tourism Impacts; Destination Carrying Capacity; Carrying Capacity Measurement; Coastal and Marine Tourism. Though this is an application oriented chapter, wherever necessary, the discussion invokes the essential aspects of theory.

The final chapter, titled *Tourism: A Community Based Approach*, is an attempt to introduce an important alternative model to tourism development. In the traditional practice, local communities remained merely as spectators or as commodities along with the other tourism products available for sale at the destination areas.

CBT achieves the socially desirable goal of managing tourism by the communities themselves. The issues discussed include: The Blueprint for Developing CBT; The Role of NGOs; Governments and CBT; and Harnessing Public-Private-Partnership. This collection of international case studies addresses the crucial issue of sustainable tourism development by asking what local communities can contribute to sustainable tourism, and what sustainability can offer communities in return.

Written in a jargon-free and engaging style, this is a student-friendly text, and is expected to be a vital introduction to this exciting, ever-changing area of study.

Babu P. George
Alexandru Nedelea

Contents

Preface *iii*

Introduction 1

1. **International Tourism: Historical Perspectives** 5
    - The Beginnings
    - Mass Tourism
    - The History of Tourism in India

2. **International Tourism: Trends** 19
    - Technological Trends
    - Tourism Post-September 11
    - Secular Trends
    - Tourism: Viability and Sustainability
    - Sustainable Development Theory: A Critique

3. **International Tourism: Contemporary Issues** 44
    - Terrorism and Tourism
    - Ecology and Tourism
    - Sex Tourism and the Gender Debate
    - Globalization, WTO, and Tourism

4. **World Geography: Concepts** 59
    - The Five Themes of Geography
    - Important Geographical Regions

- IATA Regions
- Important Tourism Destinations of India
- India: Climate and Seasons

5. **World Geography: Applications** 111
- Maps and Cartography
- Geographical Information System
- Wilderness Tourism
- Natural Parks
- Tourism Impacts
- Destination Carrying Capacity
- Carrying Capacity Measurement
- Coastal and Marine Tourism

6. **Tourism: A Community Based Approach** 150
- Community Based Development and Community Based Tourism
- Defining Characteristics of a CBT Project
- The Blueprint for Developing CBT
- The Role of NGOs
- Governments and CBT
- Harnessing Public-Private-Partnership
- Concluding Remarks

Bibliography 181

Introduction

I swim in the Tagus all across at once, and I ride on an ass or a mule, and swear Portuguese, and have got a diarrhea and bites from the mosquitoes. But what of that? Comfort must not be expected by folks that go a pleasuring.

—Lord Byron (1788-1824) British poet

Tourism is one of the fastest growing sectors of the global economy. It is an extrinsic, social phenomenon and an intrinsic, mental phenomenon. It is about the transitory movement of people across geographic and cultural landscapes for an experience of them, and the mental transformation that takes place in those who travel in that process. Thus, the nature of tourism is complex and its scope, wide. As global affluence and leisure time increases, the demand for travel and destination facilities increases, not only in degree, but also in kind. Tourism affects most countries and peoples of the world, either as hosts or guests, either positively or negatively. In parallel, while tourism changes individuals and societies the nature of tourism is changing as well.

Various definitions of tourism have been proposed

According to some, tourism is a service based industry comprising a number of tangible and intangible components. The tangible elements include transport foods and beverages, tours, souvenirs and accommodation, while the intangible elements involve education culture, adventure or simply escape and relaxation According to some others, it is an industry promoting sightseeing by people with money. Tourism is often regarded by the host community as an economic necessity but a social evil. The terms tourist and tourism were first used as official terms in 1937 by the League of Nations. Tourism was defined as people traveling abroad for periods of over 24 hours. A technically operable definition of tourism used quite frequently is that it is an all-embracing term for the movement of people to destinations away from their place of residence for any reason other than following an occupation, remunerated from within the country visited, for a period of 24 hours or more.

Hidden beneath these superficial simplicities is the truth that tourism has become a complex and multifaceted phenomenon. The multi-dimensionality of tourism phenomenon has made it difficult for any single discipline to comprehensively grasp its nuances Numerous research attempts from the parts of different disciplinary schools have enlightened aspects of tourism and have brought into its fold the much-required rigor and legitimacy. Each of these disciplinary schools incorporated methodological tools readily available with them to conduct tourism research. The differences at the level of research methods were often reflective of more fundamental differences assumed by these disciplines at ontological and epistemological levels. Anyhow, tourism knowledge remained as fragmented knowledge in tourism sociology, tourism anthropology, tourism psychology, tourism economics, tourism geography, tourism history, and so on. Among the different contributory streams to tourism, geography provides a perspective that is far superior. This is because, place is fundamental to tourism. In fact, tourism is a movement from place to place. Even the much touted futuristic idea of virtual tourism involves movement across virtual places in the cyberspace. Hence, geography, the scientific discipline that studies the socio-cultural, economic, and physical attributes of places, is sine qua non for any comprehensive understanding of tourism.

While the broad orientation of the present course is geography and international tourism, it adopts a holistic and interdisciplinary approach to the study of the social phenomenon of tourism. Community based tourism development is projected in the book as an important realization of this holistic vision. Community based tourism provides a responsible role for each stakeholder; be it the resident community at the destination, the governmental machinery, the industry, the non-governmental organizations, the academia, or, whatever. The author personally believes that the future of sustainable tourism lies in the hands of communities: the role of all other stakeholders ought to be subservient to that of the community.

While the overall objective of the course is to generate in the learner a critical consciousness of tourism, it could also become a small but important step in initiating him or her for a rewarding career in the tourism industry.

1

International Tourism: Historical Perspectives

In the middle ages people were tourists because of their religion, whereas now they are tourists because tourism is their religion

—*Robert Runcie*

This unit attempts an overview of the history of travel and tourism. Our route follows travelers from ancient times through medieval pilgrimage and the Grand Tour to the development of mass tourism. We then look at what the future holds for us.

The Beginnings

Man's travel began millennia ago with the first step of the first man in his desire to satisfy a basic need for food shelter, clothing or social interaction. The record for many of these developments is sketchy and in many cases requires extrapolation from observations of travelers that have recorded their experiences and are included them in the written record. The first roads were paths made by animals and later adapted by humans. The earliest records of such paths have been found around some springs near Jericho and date from about 6000 BC. The first indications of constructed roads date from about 4000 BC and consist of stone-paved streets at Ur in modern-day Iraq.

Affluent people have always traveled to distant parts of the world to see great buildings or other works of art, to learn new languages, to experience new cultures, or to taste new cuisine. Yet, travel in general was dangerous, expensive and a time-consuming activity that was rarely undertaken unless for business, adventure, to flee disease or war and a few other reasons, none of which leisure. Early travelers shouldn't be classified as tourists.

Means of travel included travel by foot, animal or by ship or boat. The simplest being foot, although horseback improved the pace walking did not hinder the distance one could travel. Camels, donkeys bullocks and elephants were also used whilst traveling, when using animals as transport it made the trip both expensive and allowed the traveler to carry more supplies for trade or suchlike. Early sea vessels varied from dug out tree trunks to the complex Roman galleys. According to early Western history, upper classes often traveled around the Mediterranean basin.

During the rule of Alexander the Great, 700,000 tourists visited what is now a part of Turkey. This was considerably helped by the well built and organized roads, whilst on the journey groups had the ability to change

a team of horses, stay at rest houses, and refreshments were available along the trip. During this time, the roads were crowded. Alexander the Great traveled to India and found the road systems and facilities well arranged.

It was during the same period that pleasure travel begun taking place in China and Japan. The Chinese emperor, Wu Di traveled plenty in the 2nd century. His adventures were well described in his writing.

During the reign of Elizabeth the 1st tourism reached a high. Coach travel had become popular because of its style. Young gentlemen who came from wealthy backgrounds undertook the Grand Tour in this era. They would travel to parts of Great Britain, France, and Italy, it was considered crucial for the education of the young men. The tour was used improperly on many occasions,

the youngsters would go on major shopping sprees and a lot of the time they would meet local ladies and generally behave badly.

Mass Tourism

Mass travel could not really begin to develop until the following things occurred.

- Improvements in technology allowing the transport of large numbers of people in a short space of time to places of leisure interest
- A cultural environment that nurtured the motivation to travel
- Friendly boarders, and
- Sanction to enjoy the benefits of leisure time.

The father of modern mass tourism was Thomas Cook who, on 5 July 1841, organized the first package tour in history. He arranged for the rail company to charge one shilling per person for a group of 570 temperance campaigners from Leicester to a rally in Loughborough, eleven miles away. Cook was paid a share of the fares actually charged to the passengers, as the railway tickets, being legal contracts between company and passenger, could not have been issued at his own price. There had been railway excursions before, but this one included entrance to an entertainment held in private grounds, rail tickets and food for the train journey. Cook immediately saw the potential of a convenient off the peg holiday product in which everything was included in one cost. He organized packages inclusive of accommodation for the Great Exhibition, and afterwards pioneered package holidays in both Britain and on the European continent.

He was soon followed by others (the Polytechnic Touring Association, Dean and Dawson etc.), with the result that the tourist industry developed rapidly in the late Victorian Britain. Initially it was supported by the growing middle classes, who had time off from their work, and who could afford the luxury of travel and possibly even staying for periods of time in boarding houses.

Cox & Co, the forebear of Cox & Kings, were in existence from 1758 largely entwined with the travel arrangements for the British Army serving around the Empire. While acting as 'agents' for various regiments, they organized the payment, provision, clothing and travel arrangements for members of the armed forces. In the 19th century their network of offices contained banking and also travel department. The company became heavily involved with affairs in India and its Shipping Agency had offices in France and the Middle East.

The Bank Holiday Act of 1871 introduced a statutory right for workers to take holidays, even if they were not paid at the time. By the last quarter of the nineteenth century, the tradition of the working class holiday had become firmly established in Britain. These were largely focused upon the seaside resorts.

Similar processes occurred in other countries, though at a slower rate, given that nineteenth century Britain was ahead of any other nation in the world in the process of industrialization. In the USA, the first great seaside resort, in the European style, was Atlantic City, New Jersey. In Continental Europe, early resorts included Ostend (for the people of Brussels), and Boulogne-sur-Mer (Pas-de-Calais) and Deauville (Calvados) (for Parisians).

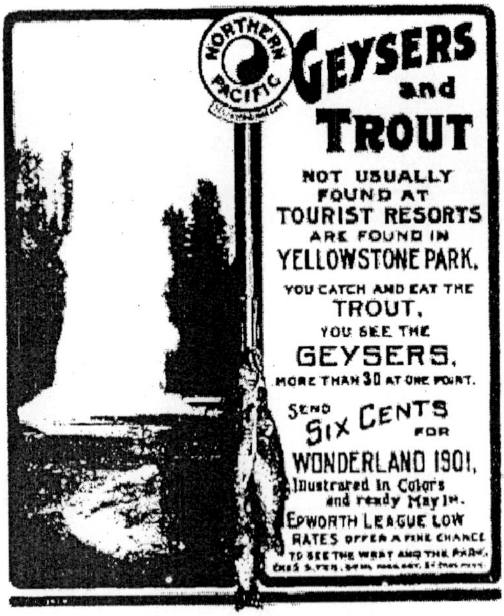

Increasing speed on railways meant that the tourist industry could develop internationally. To this may be added the development of sea travel. By 1901, the number of people crossing the English Channel from England to France or Belgium had passed 0.5 million per year. Shipping companies were anxious to fill cabin space that was under utilized. Consequently, they marketed holidays based upon sea trips from London to Lisbon and Gibraltar. Other companies diverted their older ships to operate cruises in the summer months.

However, the real age of international mass travel

began with the growth of air travel after World War Two. In the immediate post-war period, there was a surplus of transport aircraft, such as the popular and reliable Douglas Dakota, and a number of ex military pilots ready to fly them. They were available for charter flights, and tour operators began to use them for European destinations, such as Paris and Ostend. Vladimir Raitz pioneered modern package tourism when on 20 May 1950 his recently founded company, Horizon, provided arrangements for a two-week holiday in Corsica. For an all inclusive price of £32.10s.-, holiday makers could sleep under canvas, sample local wines and eat a meal containing meat twice a day - this was especially attractive due to the continuing austerity measures in post-war United Kingdom.

Nevertheless it was with cheap air travel in combination with the package tour that international mass tourism developed. The postwar introduction of an international system of airline regulation was another important factor. The bilateral agreements at the heart of the system fixed seat prices, and airlines could not fill blocks of empty seats on underused flights by discounting. But if they were purchased by a tour operator and hidden within the price of an inclusive holiday package, it would be difficult to prove that discounting had taken place - even though it was obvious that it had! This was the origin of the modern mass package tour.

Another significant development also happened at the end of this decade. The devaluation of the Spanish peseta made Spain appear a particularly attractive destination. The cheapness of the cost of living attracted increasing numbers of visitors. Spain and the Balearic Islands became major tourist destinations, and development probably peaked in the 1980s. At the same time, British tour operators developed the Algarve in Portugal. The continuing search for new, cheaper, destinations spread mass tourism to the Greek Islands, Italy, Tunisia, Morocco, parts of the coast of Turkey, and more recently Croatia.

The History of Tourism in India

Tourism in India is probably as old as its 5000 plus year old culture. India is gifted with an unending array of incredible attractions in the forms of religion and mysticism, great monuments, wildlife, ethnic-life, colorful fairs and festivals, all of which unwrapped in a stunning tapestry of the nature's grandeur as no other country in the world. There have always been movements of people from one part of the subcontinent to another and even to regions outside. Mostly, these movements were for reasons associated with pilgrimage or trade. Trade links that India has been able to maintain with other nations in the ancient, medieval, and modern world and the colorful stories being brought home about the mysterious world at the yonder-side triggered touristic imaginations of many. However, pleasure travel has by and large been limited to the elitist class. Post-medieval colonial occupation of the subcontinent by the Portuguese, Dutch, French, and the English elevated a new class of citizenry here that was in mind and soul of occidental make-up. This class, with its demonstrative zeal, has been instrumental in implanting the Western notion of tourism in India. By the second half of the 19th century, travel by sea to Great Britain, which had colonized most part of India, had gotten top priority in the vanity item list of this class. Then, like elsewhere in the world, Jet era has had a tremendous impact upon the overseas travel behavior, especially of the new industrial middle class. Yet, industrial growth and associated affluence remained in certain limited pockets; the rest of this vast country still lived in the agrarian era, till everything began to change drastically with what is popularly known as the information revolution. A great part of agrarian India took a long jump directly into the information era, almost bypassing the in-between industrial era, revolutionizing the economic landscape of the entire nation. The wiz kids are earning in dollars, pounds, and euros; they move across continents overnight on project assignments; they are the pseudo-reifications of Western cultural Diasporas in the East. The size of the Indian middle class is ever increasing. Travel for the heck of travel is affordable and in the easy reach of the neo-rich.

This much is about India as a tourism originating region. But, more than as a source of tourism demand, India is known as a supplier of tourism products and services, which is the other side of the coin. Like any other part of the world that constitutes the so called 'third world' inbound tourism began to take off much prior to its outbound counterpart in India too. Explorers from the Western Europe might have constituted only a minority; but they were charismatic individuals who could become opinion sources for a bandwagon of gaze-seeking followers. People began to travel to the East for barter trade, but in addition to commodities they brought back home exotic tales as well. European missionaries have also contributed to a great extent in the proliferation of the idea of the 'Lost East', which they exhorted should be regained for the Lord Jesus and every Christian should strive for it. This catalyzed an inflow of messianic movement to countries like India. Colonial times also saw the movement of masses of European military and administrative officers and their kith and kin to and fro India. Of course, these movements for their major part were not associated with what is called touristic pursuit, but still had important elements of it.

India has become a tempting destination for the budget conscious backpackers and the affluent sun-sea seekers to an equal measure. The great Indian exotica, like a marvelous gestalt figure, offer a multitude of meanings and readings and become everything to everybody. In the recent past, international tourist arrivals to India have grown by over 24 percent, resulting in 38 percent growth in the foreign exchange earnings. The World Travel and Tourism Council in one of its recent reports say that India is one of the largest growing tourist economies of the world. Even pessimistic estimates put the average growth rate of Indian tourism roughly at 8 percent. According to an official plan document of the Government of India, travel and tourism industry in India has an estimated potential to create 28 million new jobs in a single decade. The document forecasts that India's share of international tourist arrivals is going to skyrocket to a respectable figure of 0.62 percent by 2007 from the current figure of 0.38 percent. Government's tenth plan objective is to establish strong industry linkages with the widely acclaimed socio-economic objectives rooted in equity and sustainable development.

Coming straight to the post-industrial epoch in which we live now, tourism to the East is reinventing itself in the Western psyche as a secular pilgrimage through the lost self: the self that has been alienated in the industrial routines and has become the 'Other'. In this way, the new tourist is the seeker of a new reality: he or she does not want to experience the bad old master-slave relationship with the natives in the East, nor is there a craze to dominate over ecology and geography. The new tourist, on the contrary, is characterized by a sort of reverence to all; and, does not mind spending time and money if the same could contribute to the conservation of treasures that has already disappeared in the home society. This is indeed a paradigm shift from the traditional Western conception of mass tourism.

Along with the changes in the domestic society and domestic economy, tourism industry has also been transformed. Organized industrial activities in support of touristic movements are as sophisticated as any other industry now. The presence of multinational giants in the provision of transportation and accommodation can be seen in every major origin and destination of tourist traffic. Though the industrial production of tourist attractions is lamented as 'staged authenticity', it nevertheless exists, probably than ever before, of which virtual reality tourism is the latest exemplar. In fact, many of the technologies for these new forms of tourism, as well as for the more traditional travel and hospitality distribution system, are conceived and developed in India in its IT hubs like Bangalore and Hyderabad. Technological innovations have redefined the structure and conduct of tourism business to a great extent. In the case of India, it is to everyone's knowledge that the oligarchy of a few European tour operators controls the entire inbound tourism, thanks to the presence of a large number of small and medium scale tourism enterprises here which do not have the might to bargain. Attempts to model the business in the lines of co-operatives for collective bargaining and benefit sharing has not been successful in general. In the grave situation of the failure of the 'third way' alternatives, technology is serving the industry to raise a level-playing field. Now, even a part-time small scale tourism service provider can go online and conduct the business electronically fully bypassing the mighty intermediaries. The southern State of Kerala has been the best case in point: it resisted the muscle tactics of the middle men who controlled the European travel distribution by marketing itself directly. Now, even when tour operators advise alternative destinations, tourists compel them to provide an itinerary that includes Kerala. Now, Kerala has its place in the global tourism geography as one of the finest destinations to be seen in one's life time.

2

International Tourism: Trends

When one realizes that his life is worthless he either commits suicide or travels

—*Edward Dahlberg*

Introduction

Tourism is a dynamic super system constituted by a number of other dynamic systems. Because of this, it is difficult to predict the landscape of tourism industry for beyond a few years at the maximum.

For a long time, routines of the industrial era mechanically structured human experiences leading to the condition of alienation. Suppression of the subliminal human need for authentic experiences by the taxations of modernity led the human will to search for pre-modern objects and their symbols, even if this meant mere gazes of these objects and their symbols preserved exclusively for touristic consumption as museumized artifacts. The modern tourist is playful, permissive, spontaneous, and self-indulgent who sought a structural disjunction through the inversion of his daily roles. And this is the backdrop within which the discourse of modern tourism consumption itself is structured.

However, the face of tourism is fast changing. The postindustrial man is no longer one extra machine in a mass-production facility. Human freewill is not so much bound by the drudging rhythms of an inhuman production system as it used to be. Inventiveness has increasingly been getting embodied into the nature of work. Now the pertinent questions are: Has the postindustrial man not got fed up with the incessant and ubiquitous chaos in his work-a-day world? Does the craving for discontinuity, diversity, and change continue as the fundamental motivation for tourism in the postindustrial times as well, whose hallmark constant itself is change?

Nobody expects a quantum flip-over in the tourist attitude or behavior in an overnight. Yet, changes must have been happening in various degrees and modes for various geo-demographic and socio-psychographic segment that need to be closely watched and critically debated.

Technology Trends

Alongside, the tourism industry is also passing through an incessant process of metamorphosis. For instance, technology in tourism has become a force for radical business process reengineering. The importance of Information and Communication Technologies (ICT) as strategic, tactical, and operational tools for businesses in the new millennium, especially businesses that are in the services sector, is widely recognized. The transformation from most of the world's industrial economies into service economies has been effected by the applications ICT. Now that the dot-com boom and burst are over, realistic appraisals of the impact of technology and technological futures are being reworked in various quarters. The structure as well as the conduct of the tourism industry has been radically altered by ICT revolution.

The networked travel industry has been a very quick development and hence our knowledge about the new surroundings, the rules and exceptions of the game, are but scanty. Also, remarkable variation and fuzziness are visible while one looks at the few studies conducted in other sectors and geo-cultural regions. In the context of developing countries, there have been a lot of differences in the preparation of businesses to adopt the electronic platform across a number of variables. The larger question here is what prompts and what inhibits entrepreneurs and managers in their decision making to go electronic, which remains by and large an unexplored area.

World Tourism Organization has portrayed a vivid picture about the evolving scenario of e-tourism highlighting the following:

- Increased popularity and capabilities of the Internet for a wide spectrum of applications for electronic services in tourism, making distribution channels less dependent from traditional CRS/GDS of airlines;
- Internet and supporting services will significantly transform, if not eliminate, the role of traditional travel intermediaries (travel agents working on commission basis);
- Direct on-line bookings by customers will make up a significant market share by 2010 with access

available to most of the population in industrialized countries;

- "Virtual tourists" will have an increasing demand for multi-media travel information;
- Interactive TV and mobile devices will increasingly be used for the distribution of tourism products and services;
- The majority of tourism organizations will also use Intranets;
- Various types of smart agents supporting both tourism suppliers and customers will emerge;
- Products and services will reach a much higher level of personalization together with a corresponding demand;
- The increasing share of economically rich ageing population in the industrialized countries will affect a higher demand for e-services related to foreign travel, particularly to long haul destinations and travel for culture purposes as well as eco-tourism;
- Further growth of "time poor"—"money rich" people will entail a high demand for short time holidays while, on the other hand, all-inclusive holidays will be demanded by a large number of people with needs for complete, unburdened relaxation and release from job pressures;
- Particular uses of electronic technology will include smart cards for a variety of functions, including the management of destination loyalty schemes (discounts in exchange for customer data and loyalty), bonus schemes for environment-protective behavior, etc.;

- Internet video telephony will allow customers to take test-drives for a particular destination by pictures from cameras placed at various sites in the holiday locality and transmitted via Internet;
- Ticketing automation (satellite ticket printers) will be widespread and e-ticketing including mobile phone based forms will make up a major portion of air travel as well as railway travel during the next decade;
- Efforts to build up central databases of traveler information will be continued for use to get extensive insight into individual preferences and behavioral patterns so that the information can be used for active marketing;
- Mobile city guides will be widespread and electronic brochures in the form of CD-ROMs will increasingly replace paper brochures;
- Tourism providers will more easily and more often form e-strategic partnerships, offering complementary products;
- Small and medium sized businesses will be forced to take a more strategic approach on doing business; new mediators on the market will assist in doing so;
- Tourism regions will increasingly have to employ extensive e-based branding and marketing strategies;

Tourism Post-September 11

Since the late 2001, world tourism has been characterized by:

- A global economic downturn which affected all major economies at the same time;
- A general uncertainty after the attacks in New York and Washington followed by two wars, in Afghanistan and Iraq, and other terrorist attacks, like the one in Djerba or Bali, specifically targeting tourists; and
- Unexpected crises like the outbreak of SARS, Tsunami, which had a dramatic impact on international travel, particularly in Asia

The results are:

- Business and consumer confidence were hurt;
- There was not so much decrease in overall volume but there were above all shifts in demand;
- Major structural changes occurred in the air transport system
- There was pressure on receipts due to the "trading down" on expense
- There is a new attitude of "wait and see", resulting in late bookings;
- Trips are closer to home, to familiar destinations and there is sensitivity to price;
- Business traveling has declined: they are less and cheaper;
- Travel is organized individually, instead of going for the "organized trips": do it yourself through Internet, low cost airlines;
- For transportation, consumers prefer to travel by car, coach or train, instead of using planes;
- With regard to accommodation, apartments, country houses or similar are used instead of hotels;

- In terms of purpose of travel, consumers prefer to choose as destinations visits to family, friends or relatives (VFR)

Secular Trends

The European Travel Commission forecasts that, despite whatever differences that may continue to exist, current trends in world tourism in general favor destinations that are: safe to visit; easily accessible; with good health standards; with a developed infrastructure; and, with a clean environment. The following summarizes the ETC's findings on tourism trends:

Forecasted change	*Consequences for the tourism sector*
TRANSPORTATION:	
1. The increasing availability of high-speed trains and low-cost carriers will influence classical travel flows. 2. Road traffic will face more congestion.	1. Destinations will increasingly benefit from easy and affordable access for short breaks-in particular when major events are organized outside of the main season. 2. The increasing availability of direct links by train and plane will stimulate demand for international short breaks in cities and city regions, to the detriment of rural areas. 3. The use of high-speed trains for medium distances will take over a large proportion of the travel currently undertaken by scheduled airlines. 4. Road congestion will negatively influence transport by private car-in particular in the high season.

	5. Coach trips will decrease in importance. 6. Barriers which result from non-adapted schedules or inter-modal transportation which is not optimally connected will have a stronger negative influence on destinations that cannot meet the growing wish for easy accessibility. 7. Cruises-not only expensive cruises, but also those in 'budget-class'—will increase in popularity, in particular for those over 50 years of age.
SUSTAINABILITY	
Environmental consciousness will continue to increase. For tourism, this will result in more demand for sustainable destinations, in which nature and population will play an increasingly prominent role. In order to mitigate the costs for sustainability, the price will increasingly be passed on to the tourists themselves.	1. The regional component in destinations will increase in importance. 2. Destination management policies need to be improved through more coherent and consistent planning. 3 The preference for destinations will be more strongly connected to the support given by the local population to welcoming increasing numbers of visitors. 4. Regions which have suffered from overbuilding (particularly where this is not in keeping with the natural landscape) will increasingly be rejected as attractive destinations. 5. Eco-tourism should not be confused with sustainable tourism.
SAFETY & SECURITY	
Acts of terrorism, regional and wars, pollution and other crises have unfortunately	1. The quality of water (in lakes pools, but also of tap water) will increase in importance in the

become facts of daily life, and influence the need to feel safe and secure. In tourism, this results in an increased need for safety and security, and in tourists avoiding destinations that are perceived as unsafe.	selection of the destination, and demands better protection. 2. The more critical tourist will more quickly make claims if the product offered does not meet up to the expected standards. 3. The costs for guaranteeing safety and security will rapidly increase. 4. The industry should be better prepared to meet tourism demand more flexibly in periods of crisis.

DEMOGRAPHY

The number of persons in older age categories will rapidly increase. The average number of persons per household will decrease still further, which will result in higher disposable incomes and spending power. Seniors will be healthier and will have higher disposable incomes than in the past. Many of them will enjoy early retirement schemes. In view of this development, the number of more experienced senior travelers will increase faster than the development of tourism demand in general (although a gradual downgrading of pension benefits and a trend to increase the pensionable age may slow down this development in the long run).	1. Increasing demand for quality, convenience and security. 2. Increasing demand for easy transportation. 3. Increasing demand for more relaxing entertainment facilities (e.g. golf courses etc.). 4. Increasing demand for one-person products. 5. More demand in shoulder months. 6. In marketing, less emphasis should be put on age and more on comfort.

HEALTH

Health-consciousness will increase still further. Though increasing health-consciousness will not influence the volume of demand, it will certainly influence the deci-	1. Destinations that are perceived as less healthy will be more quickly avoided than in the past. 2. The demand for sun-holidays only will decrease still further.

sion-making with regard to destinations, and behavior during holidays.	3. Active or activity holidays will increase in popularity, and the demand for facilities that correspond to this type of holiday will be increasingly preferred. 4. The demand for 'wellness' products will increase, including spas and fitness centers.
AWARENESS & EDUCATION	
The average level of education is increasing. This will result in holidaymaking in which the arts, culture and history play a more important role, including more educational and spiritual holidaymaking.	1. Increasing demand for special products. 2. The more prominent inclusion of elements relating to the arts, culture and history in package tours and self-organized holidays. 3. The need for better and more creative communication of information. 4. Demand for new destinations in Central and Eastern Europe will increase.
LEISURE TIME	
Modern society exerts increasing pressure on peoples' daily lives, and stimulates the wish for more leisure time and relaxation-which will have an adverse effect on the increase of free disposable incomes. For tourism, this trend is thus by definition unfavorable-also because the increase in the number of days of paid leave for holidaymaking has come to a halt.	1. An increasing need to supply additional low-cost products. 2. An increasing need to offer relaxation. 3. A shortening of the longer main holiday in favor of more short ones.
TRAVEL EXPERIENCE	
More sophisticated consumers are increasingly self-	1. Alternative ways of spending time and money will

assured regarding their needs and rights. Tourists are also increasingly looking for an experience–say, the opportunity to carry out a particular activity–rather than selecting a specific destination. For tourism, this results in an increasingly critical attitude to quality, and to the price-quality ratio.

increasingly complete with holidaymaking and within holidaymaking the preferences for destinations and accommodation.

2. Destinations that do not meet up to acceptable standards will suffer more intensely, and for a longer period of time in future.
3. More mixed behavior: this holiday simple, the next one luxurious-this year long-haul, next year short-haul.
4. Holiday preference will become more fragmented in future, and thus influence repeat volumes.
5. Destination fidelity will continue to decrease over the years.
6. More experienced tourists will increasingly result in a more critical attitude to the artificial, in favor of greater authenticity-in particular with reference to emotional satisfaction and the need to personalize; artificial supply that does not distinguish itself from others (e.g. theme parks) will decrease in importance if it does not meet with higher standards.
7. Experience and critical attitudes will stimulate tourists to revisit satisfactory destinations from their travel past.
8. The increasing preference for mobility will stimulate rentals of vehicles.
9. Regions that offer a full, varied, totally balanced concept will be increasingly preferred, and will demand better destination management.

LIFESTYLES

Lifestyles in Western society change gradually. For tourism, this influences the tourist's perception of his/her personal needs and behavior.

1. Though relevant investments may be made, the interest in 'Bed & Breakfast' is lessening, since it is regarded as cheap.
2. As status is less important than it used to be, leisure behavior is becoming more personalized, leading to increased demand for smaller sized accommodation units (like smaller authentic family hotels and tourist farms).
3. The shift in perception regarding life and lifestyle results in a decline in the demand for fully escorted tours.
4. Suppliers will benefit more if they are able to create completely new products, concepts and services that distinguish themselves by their added value.
5. Increasing specialization by suppliers in relation to specific hobbies and interests will become more important, and will more often be combined with holidaymaking.
6. The increased preference for solid 'anchors' as secure holds in a more uncertain world stimulates the wish to possess second homes, also in areas close to smaller regional airports.
7. The trend of 'back to basics' results in preferences for more simple holidays: from hotel to bungalow, from caravan to tent.

INFORMATION TECHNOLOGY

The penetration of the internet-and its use for info-

1. The ready availability of tourist information on destinations and

·mation and the purchasing ɔf tourism products and ;ervices-will continue to incr- ɜase. For tourism, the role of :he internet-including new neans of visual presentation- vill increase still further, and vill prove to be of the utmost mportance in future.

products, and increasingly sophisticated search engines to analyze such information will lend itself to comparison, and thus influence competition more intensively via 'grazing'.

2. Experienced tourists will increasingly put together their own holidays on a modular basis with direct bookings.
3. The role of travel agents will decrease, as full package tours are increasingly bought directly via the net.
4. Internet will transform the classical role of the National Tourism Organizations (NTOs) and Tourist Boards at an increasing speed-but will create a new role in e-marketing, including the application of Customer Relation Management (CRM) destination marketing.
5. Destination marketing (e.g. better branding with public support) will increase in importance as the source to stimulate website visits.
6. The availability of in-depth information on suppliers' products, either on the destination site or accessible through links, will become of more importance as the basic precondition for the success of websites.
7. The possibility of 'shopping' via the internet will stimulate later bookings.
8. The growing need for secure online reservations has to be stressed in relation to more experienced and self-assured tourists.

CHANGES IN SOCIETY-
NEW WAYS OF TRAVEL

Society changes continuously, and trends–whether economic, social or lifestyle-subsequently impact on tourism, as tourism is an integral part of our society. It is important for the tourism sector to assess these changes at an early stage. Existing policies regarding products and services, marketing and investments, all demand appropriate adjustments or adaptations when preferences and behavior develop differently from the way they have done in the past. In the past, supply has always dictated demand, whereas today the reverse is true. Increasing saturation of the market and more self-assertive consumers, with more free disposable income and leisure time, determine the profitability of suppliers in the tourism sector. Competition is becoming more volatile. Although some trends are supply-funded, it is also important to forecast trends in demand, as these trends form the basis for determining the time and money required to make the relevant adjustments.

1. Increasing demand for luxury
2. Increasing demand for special products which can be obtained on impulse.
3. Increasing demand for city-breaks and other short breaks abroad-in periods that used to be less favored.
4. Higher level of interest in winter sun holidays.

For the last decade, Europe has been the theatre of a true political, social and economic revolution. The transformation of political systems and of the economies of Central and Eastern European countries, the enlargement of the European Union, the increased flow of people and goods, the introduction of a single currency in a wide area of the continent, are but a few examples of these changes. The EU enlargement will have a political impact-peace, stability and good governance, -an economic impact,-higher growth and increased welfare- and a socio-cultural impact,—increase in EU's diversity. In turn, all these elements have an impact, potentially positive, on tourism. The EU enlargement will bring benefits for the tourism industry in the entire region but in order to reap them tourism resources and skills need to be further developed.

The above trends are suggested primarily for Europe: but vigorous forces of globalization are fast sweeping away any differences that may exist across nations and continents. The trends for Europe and the developed world, thus, cannot be far different from those for the rest of the world. Even otherwise, since most of the tourists originating markets are located in the Europe and the North American continent, these trends assume a lot of practical significance.

World over, there are continuing concerns over safety and security, but it is clear that people are growing more accustomed to living in an unsafe world. The same can probably be said regarding travelers' attitudes to health risks. Tourism demand has bounced back much more quickly after the more recent terrorist attacks.

The growth in demand for low-cost airlines has been unprecedented, and it is likely to continue unabated as new carriers emerge in different regions of the world and as people continue in their search for 'good value'. But if high-speed rail becomes cheaper, it could attract passengers away from air travel, especially given the current moves to introduce aviation fuel/environmental taxes. Similarly, there will be a sharp increase in use of the internet to plan and book travel and this is expected to result in a continuation of the late-booking trend. Nevertheless, the package tour is a long way from being obsolete, even if demand is increasingly for partly packaged holidays, customized holidays and dynamic packaging, at the expense of traditional all-inclusive tour packages.

World Travel Mart (2003) Global Travel Report says that postmodernist customers are on an ever increase in tourism: it exhorts the industry to watch out for the hybrid consumer–looking to combine five-star deluxe accommodation with a low-cost flight, or opting for a fast-food dinner one evening and a slap-up meal the next.

On the global level, outbound trips rose by +5% in 2005. This growth was caused by increasing affluence, rapidly spreading low cost offers around the globe as well as by the Asian newcomers, still wanting to discover the world and having a large backlog demand for international travel. After a period of slump, the 2005 tourism statistics is to be good news, especially for the developing world: While all continents contributed to the worldwide increase in outbound trips in 2005, African destinations were at the leading edge registering a growth of +10%, followed by Asia with +7% growth. America (+6%) and Europe (+4%) also attained not so bad a growth (IPK International, 2006).

Tourism: Viability and Sustainability

The tourism sector is probably the only service sector that provides concrete and quantified trading opportunities for all nations, regardless of their level of development. However, it is also a sector where there is clearly an uneven distribution of benefits, which is threatening the social, economic and environmental sustainability of tourism in some developing countries. For many developing countries tourism is one of fundamental pillars of their development process because it is one of the dominant activities in the economy, while for others, particularly by islands and some small economies, it is the only source of foreign currency and employment, and therefore constitutes the platform for their economic development.

According to the Brundtland Commission, sustainable development is the "development that meets the needs of the present without compromising the ability of future generations to meet their own needs". It contains within it two key concepts: the concept of "needs", in particular the essential needs of the world's poor, to which overriding priority should be given; and the idea of limitations imposed by the state of technology and social organization on the environment's ability to meet present and the future needs. At an operational level, it includes the preservation and protection of diverse ecosystems- the soil, plants, animals, insects and fungi while maintaining the resource productivity by use within limits. Caring for the Earth Foundation states that sustainable development is "improving the quality of human life while living within the carrying capacity of supporting ecosystems". Simply started, this is about achieving economic and social development in ways that do not exhaust a country's natural resources.

Experts view that sustainability is inherently "inter-generational". Sustainable development should not merely be equitable development within a generation or, "intra-generational". Intra-generational equity is the principle of equity between different groups of people alive today. Inter-generational equity is the principle of equity between people alive today and future generations. The implication is that unsustainable production and consumption by today's society will degrade the ecological, social, and economic basis for tomorrow's society, whereas sustainability involves ensuring that future generations will have the means to achieve a quality of life equal to or better than today's.

The proper functioning of the tourism economy is linked to that of many other related economic activities, which accounts for the importance of its economic, social and environmental sustainability. As a matter of fact, the extent to which the business operations of international tourism, backward and forward are linked with other sectors will determine the level of performance and profitability of tourism, the extent of multiplier and spillover effects, and the retention of value added, i.e. the leakage effect. The sectors producing goods and services are linked backwards with tourism in catering for the needs of tourists and tourism operators, e.g. agriculture and food-processing industries, and other manufacturing industries providing furniture, construction materials and other articles required by tourism establishments. Similarly, many other services, such as transport, business services, financial services, professional services, construction design and engineering, environmental services, security services and government services, also ensure the efficient performance of tourism operators. Some of these sectors are also crucial for the proper linkage of tourism with foreign markets (forward linkages) because they constitute the platforms for "taking off" and for keeping the national tourism providers fully integrated with international tourism flows.

Many developing countries have found it important to improve the linking of tourism (forward and backward) with the other sectors of the economy as one of the foundations of tourism development policies, so as to capitalize on the benefits of the globalization and internationalization of markets. Successful experiences of small economies and islands that have recently become emerging tourism destinations, such as Mauritius, Maldives, the Dominican Republic and other Caribbean islands, attest to the vital importance of the proper linkage of tourism with the rest of the economy, in their capacity of retaining value added, e.g., reducing leakages. Despite developing countries efforts to develop the most suitable domestic policy environment, the economic sustainability of tourism is being undermined by external factors beyond their control, notably the predatory behavior of integrated suppliers which enjoy a dominant position in the originating markets of tourism flows.

The viability of tourism, i.e. its economic, social, cultural and environmental sustainability, is at the heart of domestic policies and development concerns of many countries in the world. For economists, viability is just the economic viability. Economists investigating the viability of tourism development in different national contexts mostly delimit their studies to: (a) the leakage effect produced by the nation's structural vulnerabilities and the difficulties in taking advantage of commercial opportunities; and (b) anti-competitive practices affecting tourism viability and performance in different segments of the tourism sector, as well as those in other sectors closely linked to travel and tourism.

Leakages from Tourism and Tourism Viability: As a modality of international commerce, tourism involves not only inflows of foreign financial resources but also outflows, referred to herein as "leakages". When they exceed specific levels, these outflows can significantly neutralize the positive financial effect of international tourism. Leakage is the process whereby part of the foreign exchange earnings generated by tourism, rather than being retained by tourist-receiving countries, is either retained by tourist-generating countries or repatriated to them in the form of profits, income and royalty remittances, repayment of foreign loans, and imports of equipment, materials, capital and consumer goods to cater for the needs of international tourist and overseas promotional expenditures.

Leakages can be divided into three categories: internal leakage or the import-coefficient of tourism activities; external leakage or pre-leakage, depending on the commercialization mode of the tourism package and the choice of airline; and invisible leakage or foreign exchange costs associated with resource damage or deterioration. A first step in reducing internal leakage is to identify what levels are appropriate given the economic structure of a country and then to ensure that effective leakage remains near this objective range while strategies to build up the local supply capacity are put in place. Although restrictive trade policies can reduce the size of the market, it is important to note that import openness tends to facilitate the leakage effect unless the economy has already in place a structure capable of reacting to the competitive stimulus of imports, which is usually not the case in the underdeveloped countries. External leakage or pre-leakage is much more difficult to measure and relates to the proportion of the total value added of tourism of services actually captured by the servicing country. To the extent that developing countries have limited access to commercialization channels in their target markets, they can only offer base prices to intermediaries that capture the mark-up on those services. Observed differences between paid and received prices for developing country tourism services (lodging, food, entertainment, etc.) suggest external leakage or pre-leakage levels of up to 75 percent. In some cases, base prices do not allow for the economic sustainability of projects, and normally do not contemplate replacement costs associated with resource depletion. This leads to problems of infrastructure and environmental sustainability, which tend to be overlooked in view of the short-term importance of crucial foreign exchange inflows. Leakage levels are not static but vary depending upon the stage of development of the tourism industry and the evolution of the economy to provide new services and products resulting from demand from the tourism sector.

Another factor to be evaluated in identifying appropriate leakage levels is the type of tourism being promoted. High-income tourism, because it requires the provision of very high quality and high priced goods, may actually result in increased leakage in some cases despite of the higher income it may generate. Mass tourism could have higher potential for leakage than ecological or adventure tourism because the latter value and consume local resources as part of the tourism experience. However, low-leakage tourism can also equate to low-income tourism, resulting in lower total income and therefore limiting the possibilities for expansion and development by other sectors of the receiving country's economy. Leakage effects on tourism net income levels are nonetheless offset by increased value added or volume.

Effects of Anti-Competitive Measures upon Tourism Viability: The competition issue and the treatment of anti-competitive behavior are at the core of the problems of efficiency, viability and sustainability of tourism in developing countries. The latter's ability to deal with those two aspects and to counter their effects is a crucial matter. Firstly, this is because anti-competitive behavior occurs largely in developed countries, as a result of the fierce competition among a few integrated dominant players with a high market share in their own market and in all segments of tourism industry supply, notably tour operators, travel agencies, hotels etc. Secondly, the pattern of globalization, which is the driving force of many of the developments in the supply of the tourism and air transport, also mostly originates and is controlled in the two leading developed economies, namely the European Union and the United States. Consequently, what often appears to be a normal commercial relationship in a developing country may actually be the result of a network of anti-competitive practices arising from a globalized and highly integrated tourism trading environment, dominated by a few suppliers in the originating tourism markets. Moreover, other non-behavior-related industry issues, such as the inadequacy or absence of a domestic competition legal framework in developing countries, and the lack of multilateral disciplines and mechanisms within the trade negotiation framework also affect the ability of developing countries to deal with or prevent anti-competitive practices in their tourism sectors.

Sustainable Development Theory: A Critique

Many sociologists, ecologists, and political scientists adopt the framework of critical theory to deconstruct the entire economic formulations associated with the term "sustainability." According to the proponents of this school, modern tourism is posited as an extension of colonialism, and they try to build a discourse on international tourism in terms dependency theory. Some critics find traces of Judaist-Christian ethic of domination and control in it. Exploration, hunting and trading dominated touristic purposes at least till mid-nineteenth century. Extractive as it is the nature of such tourism, gains were appropriated and directions of development controlled by the colonial powers and their agents. It caused a heavy depletion of ecological resources in the colonies too. Still today, tourism is remaining the privilege of the few and it may seem unbelievable that such a big multinational enterprise is there to pamper this minority: WTO forecasts that only 7% of the world population will travel abroad even by 2020. Seen hidden in the development of modern day 'adventure tourism' and 'eco-tourism' (and they may appear in different names!) is also a drive to exploit the 'exotic'. Even today, the mechanism and devices of control and access to tourist arrivals and the struggle between sending and host countries over retention of tourist expenditures are not fundamentally different. Despite being bestowed with abundant resources for natural comparative advantage, developing countries and their firms are under the mercy of the 'big' intermediaries primarily located in the North. In spite of all romanticism, the stark reality is that at the bottom line, tourism is a "business transaction, a commodity for sale in the world market. Thus, from this angle, the conventional wisdom that tourism is unambiguously good is problematized.

The issues of sustainability often lie in the competition between economic sectors for the scarce resources of land, water, energy, waste assimilation capacity etc. Each so-called stakeholder group has its own conceited interest and projects them as self-contained truths. For marketers, it is the magic magnet to attract the eco-conscious postmodern traveler who will pay anything for 'authentic', 'unadulterated' experience in the 'natural' settings. NGOs and activist groups, specializing in criticizing but without alternative solutions, find in it great sources of funding and they will be happiest if such issues are ever burning. There is nothing but ideologies- 'economic' on the one extreme and 'ecological' on the other and a whole lot of 'perspectives' in between. One of the oft-quoted reports prepared by the UN World Commission on Environment and Development under the chairmanship of Gro Harlem Bruntland (entitled "Our Common Future") tacitly espouses the paradigm of postindustrial market philosophy. It heralds what according to its authors is "growth imperative" as the key to ensuring both intra and inter-generational equity. A white paper from the World Tourism Organization, released in July 2002, wants to "encourage the rapid expansion of tourism in line with market capacity", again through "progressive liberalization". Some opponents see these as legitimization exercises undertaken for the trans-national behemoths that deplete the scarce resources of the world, both natural and cultural, making the life of the vast majority of people living mostly in developing and under developed countries miserable and they call for a qualitatively different conceptualization as well as praxis of development.

Worldview of the developed West (centered on the self-centered, behavior of the rational 'animal' only through the market clearing price) stresses the development part of Sustainable Development while the eastern worldview in general attaches a lot of importance to the sustainability part independent of whether such an approach leads to development or not in the strict material sense of the term. Tourism theoreticians, especially the sociological school, tries to take a middle path in an attempt to be comprehensive and for them sustainable tourism is that which is developed and maintained in a form such that it is viable over an indefinite period and does not degrade or alter the physical and human environment to an extent that it prohibits the successful development and well being of other activities and processes. The mayhem, according to some authors, lie in our failure in appreciating in totality the diverse conceptions that different communities hold- worldviews that are gestalts which effectively prohibit attempts to compound those conceptions (each of which meaningful to at least the members of the espousing community) in to a richer and more encompassing reality. A posture like this, probably, would be much more digestible to the ecological school than the economic counterpart that feel more at ease with its accurate, scientific and well defined goals and quantitative methods to reach them. The minimum background material given above is only to suggest that the complexity involved in constructing knowledge in different contextual frames make the entire debate on sustainable tourism extremely problematic, especially since stake holding communities are spread across continents and cultures.

3

International Tourism: Contemporary Issues

Tourism is like fire: you can cook your dinner on it, but if you are not careful it will burn your house down. If you harness it, it can heat your home and cook your food forever.

—*Anonymous*

Tourism encompasses an intricate array of relationships between the various systems and subsystems in the society. There exists almost no aspect of social life where its scope of association and impacts are not present. Thus, tourism is invariably a matter of debate and discussion in different spheres of life. This means, given a free ride, a chapter on contemporary issues in tourism can lead to thousands of pages of documented text. However, in the present unit, we take up a few hot topics on tourism that are debated utmost frequently and seriously.

Terrorism and Tourism

Tourism is considered as a fragile industry in that it is

highly susceptible to external shocks such as wars, famines, natural disasters, outbreak of contagious diseases, terrorism, and so on. The impact of terrorism on a state's economy may be enormous, leading to unemployment, homelessness, deflation, crime and other economic and social ills. The contribution of tourism and travel to both industrialized and developing countries is now so great that any downturns in the level of activity in the industry are a cause of concern. The repercussions extend beyond activities directly associated with tourism, notably airlines, hotels and catering, to sectors that supply intermediate or final goods that are purchased by firms and employees in the industry.

Before September 11th (the day terrorists hit the World Trade Centre in the USA), travel and tourism was the world's largest industry, accounting for one in every 12 jobs. In 2001 until September, the global travel industry had achieved a slight growth in the number of international tourist arrivals compared to the last few years. When the massive $3.6 trillion industry almost ground to a halt after the terrorist attacks, the ripple effects extended well beyond the United States, exposing the vulnerability of countries too dependent on international tourism. The aftermath of September 11 has shown us how important travel and tourism are to the global economy and also how over-dependence on tourism can devastate lives and derail economies. This much is unbearable: even in the best of times, the consequences of tourism's rapid growth have not always been positive. On average, as much as 50 percent of tourism earnings ultimately leak out of the developing world-in the form of profits earned by foreign-owned businesses, promotional spending abroad, or payments for imported goods and labor. And uncontrolled tourism development-on mountaintops, along coastlines, or in remote jungle areas-stresses many fragile ecosystems and cultures.

However, the impact of terrorism upon tourism need not be a permanent retardation in tourism demand, especially if terrorist activities can be contained from spreading as a regular and omnipresent phenomenon. This is because tourism is so fundamental a need that it cannot be set aside by a few terrorist attacks here and there. However, risk averse people may stop to travel to unfamiliar destinations. In a study conducted recently by the author of the present book, it has been revealed that the "sense of place" and "place attachment" are important variables that decide one's decision to visit a disaster hit destination. Those who feel a sense of attachment to a destination, especially emotional attachment, do not mind visiting a risk-prone destination.

A related debate is, whether, in a terror-savaged world, given an opportunity to experience the authentic touristic reality sitting in front of a technology mediated environment at home (cyber-tourism), will people still travel physically to dangerous locations in the physical world? But, this issue is more of futuristic nature and is not debated here any further.

Also, terrorism and other disasters, for good or bad, have attracted a large number of tourists to the affected destinations. This phenomenon, coming under the category of disaster tourism, (thana tourism and dark tourism are two related terms, sometimes used alternatively), though beneficial in reinvigorating the local economy, has received criticism from NGOs and other agencies involved in recovery activities. They complain that tourists obstruct the rehabilitation efforts. Tourists, gazing at the affected people with touristic expressions, may amplify the psychological trauma of the affected people as well.

Tourists are often the targets of terrorist groups and even Luddites who do not want any change. For the former, tourists represent the cream of the developed society which is to be eliminated at any cost; and, for the latter tourism is a vital weapon of globalization to bring about changes and flatten the historical forces. Sophisticated terrorists constantly evaluate their present status, which may be considered as either satisfying or unsatisfying. If satisfying, a terrorist group may accept the status quo. If unsatisfying, a terrorist group might recognize that goals are at risk and make changes. If a terrorist group elects to make changes, it will expect new outcomes. For them, attacking tourists is an important means to bring the international media and civil society attention and their by to pressurize to pass their demands. To contain the terrorist threat, many suggestions have been proposed. Some of them are: states should push for international recognition of tourist terrorism. There should be an international treaty denouncing terrorism that targets tourism. Also, states should seek to internalize the concepts like the "right to tourism," "liberty of tourist movements," and "rights of the workers and entrepreneurs in the tourism industry." These concepts should be integrated into domestic law, the violations of which would carry fines and prison sentences. The international community should support the development of a inter-governmental organization that focuses on tourism and terrorism somewhat along the lines of the International Court of Justice.

Ecology and Tourism

Ecology is vital to the "New Tourism" phenomenon. Ever since significant demand for nature-based tourism options have been noticed, studies have been commissioned to look into the impacts of tourism upon the ecology of a natural region. Many concluded that tourism development is invariably damageous to ecology. The other side argued that properly introduced, tourism can contribute to the ecological well-being. The latter group defined ecotourism as responsible travel to natural areas which conserves the environment and sustains the livelihood of local people.

Worldwide, ecotourism (ET) is the tourism industry's fastest growing sub-sector, with an estimated annual growth of 10-15%. Some estimates suggest that 20% of all international tourists are in some way involved in ecotourism. According to the World Wildlife Fund for Nature, 20% of the revenue generated from tourism in developing countries is due to ecotourism. ET activities are offered by a large and wide variety of operators, and practiced by an even larger array of tourists. Because ecotourism is primarily resource-based, protection of these natural and cultural resources is essential for sustained ecotourism. Many conservation organizations and governments see ecotourism as the means to both preserve and develop natural and cultural resources in the remote areas.

While there are a number of sustainable tourism options cited in the literature ecotourism is the most debated among these, and it has become almost customary to use the term 'ecotourism' as a generic substitute for all types of sustainable tourism options. This is a significant movement away from the traditional conception of ET as tourism in natural areas. The broader conception of ecotourism as a faithful operationalization of sustainable tourism principles is widespread. Sustainable tourism has emerged in response to the increasing negative impacts of ill- conceived and unplanned mass tourism activities and can be classified into:

- Natural—adventure tourism, ecotourism, and nature tourism
- Cultural—archaeological, rural, religious and ethnic
- Events—sports, carnivals, festivals, etc.
- Others—educational/health/medical/space tourism.

It is true that, Ill-conceived, improperly planned, and uncontrolled tourism activities would adversely affect the natural as well as cultural resources. . However, tourism industry has grater reasons to conserve/protect the diversity and quality of the natural and cultural resources of the destination areas, on which it ultimately thrives. The linkages between tourism, ecology, economics, culture, and livelihoods are inseparable and cut across several sectors; however, intangible costs and benefits (due to environmental and social-economic-cultural impacts) are rarely understood and appreciated in the right vein. Though it is well known that 'environment is the travel industry's base product', it is rarely respected by the tourism promoters. While many tourism promotion efforts banner the climate, sun, warmth, and sand of particular coastal destinations, tourism's dependency on environments, in particular, nature-dominated environments, does not appear to be well understood within the tourism and recreation industry. This dependence is discussed only in the academic literature, the language of which is inaccessible to the planners and policymakers. Important entries in the environmental management lexicon such as monitoring and coordination, carrying capacity, ecological foot prints, and sustainability are rarely understood and appreciated by the tourism industry, the planners, or the implementing agencies in India. Very often we focus more on how the tourism industry is meeting its legal obligations for environmental protection (such as emissions) than the dependency of tourism on high-quality natural environments.

The tourism sector in countries like India is characterized by a diversity of stake-holders, with mixed priorities, but with lack of communication and coordination and with 'mutual mistrust', tending toward a 'tragedy of the commons'—overexploitation of the commons (e.g. ground water, bio resources on common lands, etc.), degradation of biodiversity, erosion of culture and heritage, and so on. The conflicts between human economic security and ecological integrity are getting graver than ever before. Thus, the tourism and recreation industry are confronted with really difficult choices about their future. The decisions made now will for decades not only affect the local habitats and ecosystems but also the lifestyles and economic opportunities of residents in tourism destination areas. Many of these decisions are proved to be irreversible because once habitats/ ecosystems/communities lose the character that makes them distinctive and attractive to tourists, they lose their ability to vie for tourist-based income in an increasingly competitive marketplace.

Hence, we need to work towards integrated and sustainable approaches to enhance the mutually reinforcing linkages, rather than falling preys to ad-hoc, cornucopian approaches. Worldwide, tourism is undergoing a fundamental change, from the experiences and settings travelers demand to the regulations governments impose to protect the environment. Some signs of these shifts are available from elsewhere, ranging from the changing perception of the industry statements on the value of the environment to the consumer demand for sustainable tourism options.

Sex Tourism and the Gender Debate

Sex tourism is tourism, partially or fully for the purpose of having sex, often with prostitutes. Sex tourists, also called mongerers and sexpats, are adults who travel in order to have sexual relations with another adult often for the exchange of money or presents. Sometimes, pedophiles who travel to have sex with children at the destination areas are also included in the category of sex tourists. Sex tourism is at the centre stage of a wider debate on gender and tourism.

As leisure time and wealth increase, tourism consumption also increases As expansion reaches the remotest corners of the world, the marketing and consumption models between guests and hosts have indicated several possibilities for gender analysis. Power, control and equality in tourism are articulated through race, class and gender in the practice of tourism. Men and women through interconnected economic, political, cultural, social and environmental dimensions are involved in different ways in the construction and consumption of tourism. It is the recognition of these differing realities that shape tourism marketing, tourist motivation, and resident action. This process may be called the creation of stereotypes. For example, in all Asian societies where traditional society is intersecting with global economic systems, we have seen that the major public role of women in the tourism industry is in sex tourism. The faster the process of liberalization and globalization, the greater it is the spread of sex tourism.

Researchers in the feminist tradition point out that if tourism is seen as an activity that depends on leisure time and disposable income, then the enabling conditions are hierarchical and influenced by class and global economic strengths. In tourism advertising women are seen as passive, available and dependent. Women are thus sexual and exotic markers in the tourism brochure. Destinations reinforce this stereotype. Tourism, like other activities, perpetuates the international and domestic division of labor, too (Rao, N. 2001). This means that there are gendered employment activities as well as control of waged work. There is also no computation of unpaid labor by women. Feminists also criticize the construction of tourism in such a way as to preserve the "naturalness", conveniently defined as male dominated tradition.

There is another side to what have so far been discussed: "Romance on the Road: Traveling Women Who Love Foreign Men", a book by Jeannette Belliveau explores the reasons so many women have plunged into the hedonistic world of sex tourism and the risks and rewards they face in their hunt for pleasure, healing and love. Many women while on travel exploit male sex workers and "buy" their bodies for touristic consumption. Though hundreds of thousands of women have indulged in holiday liaisons, their behavior still remains one of the last remaining taboos.

Sex tourism is found to have connections with the proliferation of anti-social activities in destination areas. It often creates a parallel system of governance. Sex tourism is condemned for the fact that it has the potential to ruin traditional institutions and belief systems.

Globalization, WTO, and Tourism

Beginning with the migration of human beings out of Africa, travel has always been central to human history. While the mass tourism and leisure industry only originated in the nineteenth century, pilgrimage and other forms of travel for non-commercial purposes existed in most societies. Today, the desire to travel and to be a tourist is practically universal, and touristic practices pervade many areas of social life. Tourism has been a central dimension of globalization, and it offers a useful lens on many key questions about where globalization is taking us: questions about identity and heritage, commoditization, historical and cultural representation, authenticity and ownership, neo-liberalism, inequality, gender relations, environmental sustainability, and more.

Globalization means the development of extensive worldwide patterns of socio-cultural and economic relationships between nations. The increasing world-wide integration of markets for goods, services and capital that attracted special attention in the late 1990s is one of the hallmarks of globalization. Globalization refers to a variety of other changes that were perceived to occur at about the same time, such as an increased role for large corporations (MNCs) in the world economy and increased intervention into domestic policies and affairs by international institutions such as the IMF, WTO, and the World Bank. This process has led to the creation and operation of global tourism market where destinations, which are expected to compete on equal basis regardless of the country of origin, function interactively. Creation of a global society means that tourism businesses have the ability to operate globally and many have opted for a competitive strategy of internationalization.

In tourism, globalization affects the supply and demand side in many ways. The important supply factors are: worldwide acting suppliers, as well as the impact of computerized information and reservation systems; decreasing costs of air travel and the possibilities of having access to destination with relatively low price and income levels, as well as relatively low social standards; emerging new destinations. Important demand factors for globalization are: increasing income and wealth; tourists are more experienced and knowledgeable. The characteristics of globalization in tourism are summarized in terms of the following factors:

Economy:

- Horizontal and vertical integration strategies of tourism enterprises
- Foreign investment in hotels and tourist attractions
- Global players and strategic alliances
- Global tourism management
- Global competition of holiday resorts

Technology:

- Global booking systems
- Standardized technologies in transport systems

Culture:

- Global tourist: uniform traveler behavior
- Creation of global tourist village

Ecology:

- Tourism as global syndrome of ecology problem
- Climate changes and their effects on destinations

Politics:

- Increasing importance of international tourism organizations
- Necessity for global coordination and regulation of passenger circulation
- Sustainable development as quality and dominant idea

While WTO negotiations mainly focused on the manufacturing sector, more tourism specific issues come under the General Agreement on Trade in Services (GATS). The full liberalization of tourism services should be in principle a win-win situation for all but for the predatory practices of few dominant suppliers in the world tourism markets. Realizing that, irrespective of whether it is 'right' or 'wrong', our decision makers have determined to take the world through the path of free trade, the best possible course of action for us is to fulfill those range of conditions that ensure at least a fairer role for the affected groups: These include access to investment and technology especially for web-commerce that is a great leveler as well as curative systems for the bourgeoning negative impacts from international tourism, existence of an adequate policy, regulatory and institutional infrastructure, and the human capacity to understand where the openings lie and how they may be exploited. Governments should recognize that GATS process has as its one face a one-way street toward increased limitations on environmentally and socially responsible policies. Once countries adopt increased commitments in particular sectors, it is virtually impossible to reverse course. Countries can list limitations on their commitments, but once they have done so, they can only increase those limitations or reverse a commitment altogether after waiting three years and then providing compensation (by liberalizing another sector!). For developing countries in particular, such rules will tie a government's hands in dealing with transnational investors and their self-seeking policies and practices.

Responsible tourism advocates caution that, to ensure sustainable tourism development in the globalized world, each of us should:

- Prove and exemplify that sustainability issues offer one and the only means for developing truly sustainable international tourism business and not a barrier to be overcome by the trade through lobbying and vicious means.
- Frame guidelines for future negotiations in such a way that while them implemented, only sustainable use of touristic resources and greater equity shown by the business community result in profit. And, this is one of the best ways for trade liberalization efforts to regain the lost legitimacy too.
- Ensure that the rounds of negotiations are open not just to those holding narrow commercial interests only but also to all legitimate parties including governmental tourism bodies (NTOs) and their inter governmental (IGOs) counterparts, destination and attraction owners, intermediaries like travel agents and tour operators, accessibility and amenity providers, representatives of the labor

force, local communities at the destinations and NGOs and other grassroots level organizations.

- Demand commitment and cooperation of suppliers of air, land and maritime infrastructure, construction and management services, and other entities, in the sustainable development programs of international and regional organizations.
- Ensure that international trade negotiations are not carried out in isolation and do not undermine concerted efforts in multiple forums to promote sustainable development thereby preventing conflicting legal obligations for governments.
- Demand for the establishment of local chapters within the WTO regime with reasonable autonomy to take into account local priorities and concerns and incorporate them into a wider bottom-up framework.
- Provide educational and training drives aimed at the third world to enable or empower them to take advantage of more open trade. Awareness programs in the areas of Gender equitability and related issues should also be designed.
- Encourage the inclusion of gender and various sorts of disability voices and their representatives of the civil society at various stages in the negotiation process.
- Ensure that trade policy issues do not impose themselves into other policy areas that are weaker and less market supported but better reflecting the essence of human culture.
- Lobby for a special annex on tourism since heterogeneity of the industry makes it virtually

impossible to monitor progressive liberalizatioı and its impacts. One probable solution is a cluste approach modifying the World Tourisn Organization's Tourism Satellite Account (TSA) This will, in addition, will not fundamentall thwart 'negotiate as a package' requirement.

GATS schedules are still grossly untested and th complexity involved in the provision of tourism service (since they include commitments across sectors and eveı within specific sectors, include commitments to service the providers of services, and the way in which th service is provided) makes the chances of wron calculations much probable. Contingent factor that migh get in the way have the power to redirect the entir trajectory. Browsing literature across time might reve to a discerning reader that the debates on GATS and i impacts have gone through a radical shift in the pos September 11. Diverse conceptions of terms and the practical realizations in different communities, culture and stakeholder groups can bind the scope of an dominant and consensual design among reactionar groups and in which case this Achilles' heel will be th greatest boon for the post colonial super states and the trans-national giants.

4

World Geography: Concepts

The routines of tourism are even more monotonous than those of daily life

—*Mason Cooley*

Introduction

Geography is the science of place and space. Geographers ask where things are located on the surface of the earth, why they are located where they are, how places differ from one another, and how people interact with the environment.

There are two main branches of geography: human geography and physical geography. Human geography is concerned with the spatial aspects of human existence—how people and their activity are distributed in space, how they use and perceive space, and how they create and sustain the places that make up the earth's surface. It is human geographers who mostly work in the field of tourism. Human geography provides an understanding of the social and economic relationships that exist in providing tourism and recreation opportunities and activities, as well as the special meaning that these places have to individuals. They can also be found involved in urban and regional planning, transportation, marketing, real estate, and international business. Physical geographers, on the other hand, study patterns of climates, land forms, vegetation, soils, and water. They forecast the weather, manage land and water resources, and analyze and plan for forests, rangelands, and wetlands. However, it is to be noted that physical geography provides the essential background against which tourism places are created. Geographers also study the linkages between human activity and natural systems. According to the American Association of Geographers (AAG), geographers were, in fact, among the first scientists to sound the alarm that human-induced changes to the environment were beginning to threaten the balance of life itself.

Geography is fundamental to the study of tourism because tourism is geographical in nature. Tourism Geography is the study of travel and tourism as an industry, as a human activity, and especially as a place phenomenon. From a geographical point of view, tourism consists of the places of tourist origin (or tourist generating areas), tourist destinations (or places of tourism supply), and the relationship (connections) between origin and destination places, which includes transportation routes, business relationships, and traveler motivations.

The Five Themes of Geography

The five themes of geography were formulated by the Joint Committee on Geographic Education of the National Council for Geographic Education (NCGE) and the

Association of American Geographers (AAG) in the year 1984.

Theme 1: Location

Every point on Earth has a specific location that is determined by an imaginary grid of lines denoting latitude and longitude. Parallels of latitude measure distances north and south of the line called the Equator. Meridians of longitude measure distances east and west of the line called the Prime Meridian. In other words, latitude measures the North-South direction and longitude measures the East-West direction. Geographers use latitude and longitude to pinpoint a place's absolute, or exact, location. Combining latitude and longitude results in a grid that covers the globe. Every point can be defined by a north/south degree and an east/west degree.

For example, Seattle, Washington, USA is at latitude 47.6° North and longitude 122.33° West. From the center of the earth, look up 46.6° from the equator and turn right (west) 122.33° from the Prime Meridian and you will be looking right at Seattle.

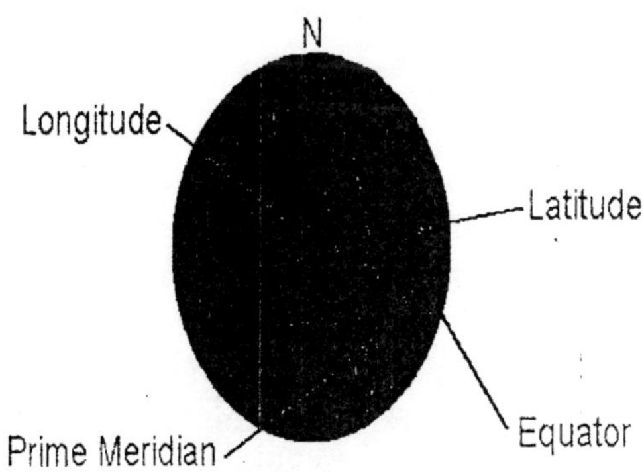

As the earth is almost 25000 miles around, dividing that into 360 pieces means each degree is about 69 miles wide around the equator, which is not very precise. To help with that, each degree is divided into 60 minutes and each minute is divided into 60 seconds.

Some tips to remember about latitudes and longitudes:

- As a convention, latitude is always given before longitude (49° N 100° E)
- Latitudes are parallel, but longitudes are not
- Degrees West and South are sometimes referred to as negative degrees (-12° -23° is the same as 12 S 23 W)
- A place's latitude affects its climate, but not its longitude
- Key longitude lines are the Prime Meridian (o°) and the International Date Line (180°)
- Key latitude lines include the equator (0°), tropic of cancer (23°26′ N), tropic of capricorn (23°26′ S), the arctic circle (66°33′ N), and the antarctic circle (66°33′ S)

Theme 2: Place

All places have characteristics that give them meaning and character and distinguish them from other places on earth. Geographers describe places by their physical and human characteristics. Physical characteristics include such elements as animal life. Human characteristics of the landscape can be noted in architecture, patterns of livelihood, land use and ownership, town planning, and communication and transportation networks. Languages, as well as religious and political ideologies, help shape he character of a place. A destination's sense of place, often leading to place attachment, is often a key element ehind tourism development: after all, without the iniqueness and diversity of places, tourism would be nundane and uninteresting.

Theme 3: Human/Environment Interaction

The environment means different things to different people, depending on their cultural backgrounds and echnological resources. In studying human-environment nteraction, geographers look at all the effects, positive nd negative, that occur when people interact with their urroundings. Sometimes a human act, such as damming river to prevent flooding or to provide irrigation, equires consideration of the potential consequences. The onstruction of a boating facility, for example, change the atural landscape, but it may also create a reservoir that elps provide water for an arid region. Studying the onsequences of human-environment interaction helps people plan and manage the environment responsibly.

Theme 4: Movement

People interact with other people, places, and things lmost every day of their lives. They travel from one place o another; they communicate with each other; and they ely upon products, information, and ideas that come from eyond their immediate environment. In that process, the nfluence becomes mutual. Studying movement and its onsequences is fundamental to tourism geography.

Theme 5: Regions

A basic unit of geographic study is the region, an area n the earth's surface that is defined by certain unifying haracteristics. The unifying characteristics may be physical, human, or cultural. In addition to studying the unifying characteristics of a region, geographers study how a region changes over times. Using the theme of regions, geographers divide the world intc manageable units for study.

Important Geographical Regions

Geographical features have a tremendous impact on the tourism flows. A geographical region is a demarcated area of the Earth. One most common way of classifying is that in terms of continents.

The word "continent" is originated from Latir "continere" for "to hold together. In general opinion there are a maximum of seven continents - Africa Antarctica, Asia, Australia/Oceania, Europe, North America, and South America. Africa, the Americas Antarctica, Asia, Australia together with Oceania, and Europe are considered to be Continents, according to some other classifications. Some geographers and scientists now refer to six continents, where Europe and Asia are combined (because they're one solid landmass) The alternative names being in use for some of the continents are: "Latin America" for South America "New World" for North America; "Occident", fo Europe; and, "Orient", for Asia.

The term continent is used to differentiate between the various large areas of the earth into which the land surface is divided. So, a continent is a large, continuou area of land on Earth. All continents together constitute less than one-third of the earth's surface, which mean more than two-thirds of the earth's surface are covered with water. Two-thirds of the continental land mass i located in the Northern Hemisphere.

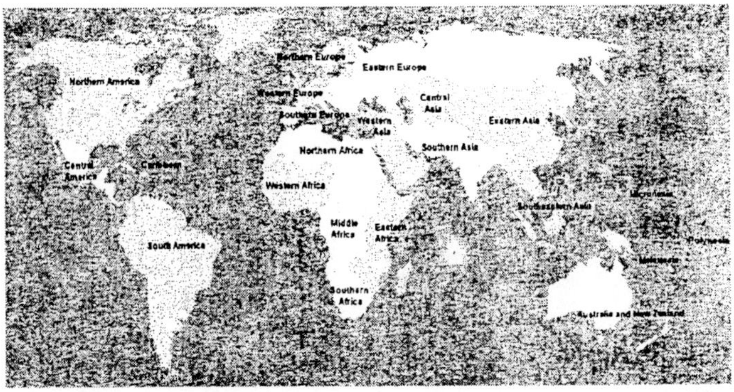

The composition of the geographic regions of the world as classified by the United Nations Statistics Division is given below:

001 World

002 Africa

014 *Eastern Africa*

017 *Middle Africa*

015 *Northern Africa*

018 *Southern Africa*

011 *Western Africa*

019 Americas

419 Latin America and the Caribbean

029 *Caribbean*

013 *Central America*

005 *South America*

021 Northern America

142 Asia

143 Central Asia

030 Eastern Asia

034 Southern Asia

035 South-Eastern Asia

145 Western Asia

150 Europe

151 Eastern Europe

154 Northern Europe

039 Southern Europe

155 Western Europe

009 Oceania

053 Australia and New Zealand

054 Melanesia

057 Micronesia

061 Polynesia

Selected economic and other groupings

... Developed and developing regions

199 Least developed countries

432 Landlocked developing countries

722 Small island developing states

778 Transition countries

Notes:

1. The designation sub-Saharan Africa is commonly used to indicate all of Africa except northern Africa, with the Sudan included

in sub-Saharan Africa.

2. The continent of North America (003) comprises Northern America (021), Caribbean (029), and Central America (013).

3. There is no established convention for the designation of "developed" and "developing" countries or areas and available classifications are contentious. In common practice, Japan in Asia, Canada and the United States in northern America, Australia and New Zealand in Oceania, and Europe are considered "developed" regions. In international trade statistics, the Southern African Customs Union is also treated as a developed region and Israel as a developed country; countries emerging from the former Yugoslavia are treated as developing countries; and countries of Eastern Europe and of the Commonwealth of Independent States (code 172) in Europe are not included under either developed or developing regions.

4. "Countries in transition from centrally planned to market economies" is a grouping used for economic analysis.

Now, let us see each of the continents in more depth:

Africa

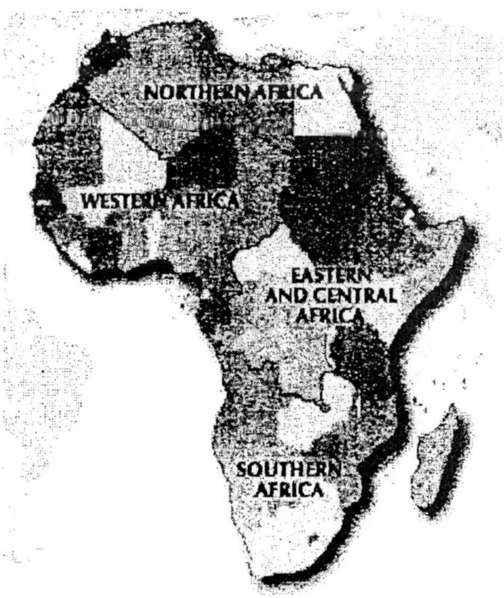

Africa is located in the Southern Hemisphere. Africa is the world's second-largest and second-most populous continent, after Asia. It consists of 4 regions: Northern Africa, Western Africa, Eastern and Central Africa, and Southern Africa. It is separated from Europe by the Mediterranean Sea and is joined to Asia at its northeast extremity by the Isthmus of Suez.

The climate of Africa ranges from tropical to subarctic on its highest peaks. Its northern half is primarily desert or arid, while its central and southern areas contain both savanna plains and very dense jungle (rainforest) regions. In between, there is a convergence of these two.

Africa is the oldest inhabited territory on earth, with the human species originating from the continent. About 3300 BC, the historical record opens in Africa with the rise of literacy in the Pharaonic-ruled civilization of Egypt, which continued, with varying levels of influence over other areas. In the mid nineteenth century European and particularly British explorers became interested in exploring the heart of the continent and opening the area for trade, mining and other commercial exploitation. This colonial occupation continued until after the conclusion of World War II, when all the colonial states gradually obtained formal independence. Today, Africa is home to 53 independent countries, which mostly still have the borders drawn during the era of European colonialism. Due largely to the effects of colonialism, corrupt governments and despotism, Africa is the world's poorest inhabited continent, too.

Africa has a number of overlapping cultures, with several thousand ethnic groups. Africans profess a wide variety of religious beliefs, with Christianity and Islam being the most widespread, though the indigenous

African religions tend to revolve around animism and ancestor worship. It is the most polyglot continent in the world as well. There are four major language families native to Africa: Afro-Asiatic, Nilo-Saharan, Niger-Congo, and Khoisan. Yet, in numerous countries, English and French are used for communication in the public sphere such as government, commerce, education and the media. Many African languages are tone languages, in which pitch level determines the meaning. This also finds expression in African musical melodies and rhythms.

The following is the list of countries in Africa:Algeria

Angola Benin
Botswana Burkina Faso
Burundi Cameroon
Cape Verde Central African Republic
Chad Comoros
Congo, Democratic Republic of the
Congo, Republic of the Cote d'Ivoire
Djibouti Egypt
Equatorial Guinea Eritrea
Ethiopia Gabon
Gambia, The Ghana
Guinea Guinea-Bissau
Kenya Lesotho
Liberia Libya
Madagascar Malawi
Mali Mauritania
Mauritius Morocco
Mozambique Namibia
Niger Nigeria
Rwanda Sao Tome and Principe
Senegal Seychelles

Sierra Leone	Somalia
South Africa	Sudan
Swaziland	Tanzania
Togo	Tunisia
Uganda	Western Sahara
Zambia	

Zimbabwe Governments in Africa are found to be showing increasing interest in promoting tourism as a source for growth and diversification. Although started from a lower base of arrivals, the African continent is on a sustainable growth path with over 7% growth per year. Recent trends in the travel and tourism industry indicate that potential travelers are becoming more aware of the wide diversity of people and environments in Africa, which is unequalled in any other location in the world, from its fantastic wildlife and natural landscapes to its fascinating and cultural historical heritage. However, with the global tourism industry going ultra-competitive with very thin margins on packaged mass-holidays, Africa has to seriously think of niche marketing the abundant alternative tourism products that it has got. Providing enough safety and security for the traveling public is a condition that tour operators insist now given that under the EU legislation they are accountable for the same to the customers. Certain perceptions, whether real or imaginary, have dealt a crippling blow to the travel and tourism industry of Africa. As a result, many airlines have been facing serious financial difficulties; the hotel and hospitality industry are being severely affected; and, people are increasingly putting off overseas travel.

According to the WTTC, one of the fastest growing

trends in tourism in the world is adventure travel, although this description can cover a wide variety of interests. The African Continent possesses some of the greatest deserts, beaches, tropical rainforest, and mountain ranges in the world and beckons the adventure tourist to come visit, explore and enjoy. Most adventure tourism activities are, however, not for the timid and are specifically aimed at those tourists who wish to break away from stereotypical vacations. Classic examples of this range from a climbing expedition of Mount Kilimanjaro, which is a popular trek for serious visitors to Tanzania to the more recent airborne adventure of hot air ballooning over and/or bungee jumping from Victoria Falls in Zimbabwe. With regard to the nature lover, there are also the awesome natural environments with the widest range of animals and plant life found on the planet including many unspoiled Eco-systems yet to be discovered. Many public-private joint efforts have been made to preserve these natural wonders and impart as little as possible negative impact on the environment. Classic examples of this range from the wildlife conservation programs of the world famous Serengeti in East Africa, to the Okavango Delta in Botswana, to the isolated and unique Eco-system of Madagascar.

Unquestionably, Africa is without a doubt a land of great historical interest as well as a place where different stages of the history of mankind can be seen - sometimes in still existing cultures. Many of these cultural sites are equipped with facilities and organized tours so that the interested visitor can have a first-hand experience of the location and cultural diversity of the area, often helping to support the welfare of the local people and the preservation of the significant cultural and historical sites nearby where they live. In addition, local arts and crafts represent a rapidly expanding area of the cultural tourism industry that create small businesses and jobs for many Africans as well as increases export market potential of many African nations. Examples of this range from the various cultural and historical sites of Nigeria to the timeless land of the Masai in Tanzania and Kenya.

In summary, Africa is truly an immense, diverse and endlessly fascinating continent and the travel and tourism industry of Africa offers unlimited potential for economic growth and opportunity. Given the great diversity of tourism attractions and the commitment of progressive policies being channeled in this lucrative industry by many African nations, the future of tourism in Africa looks very promising.

Antarctica

Encompassing the entire South Pole, Antarctica is located

in the southern most part of the world and is nearly uninhabited. It is surrounded by the Southern Ocean and divided by the Transantarctic Mountains. Antarctica means "opposite to the Arctic," the Earth's northernmost region.

It is the coldest and the driest and the windiest and the highest continent on earth. Only cold-adapted plants and animals can survive there. There are no permanent human residents and Antarctica has never had an indigenous population. The Antarctic Treaty was signed in 1959 by 12 countries. The treaty prohibits military activities and mineral mining, supports scientific research, and protects the continent's eco-zone. There is no indigenous government in Antarctica. The management of the Antarctic is organized through the legal framework of the Antarctic Treaty. Forty-three nations are now party to

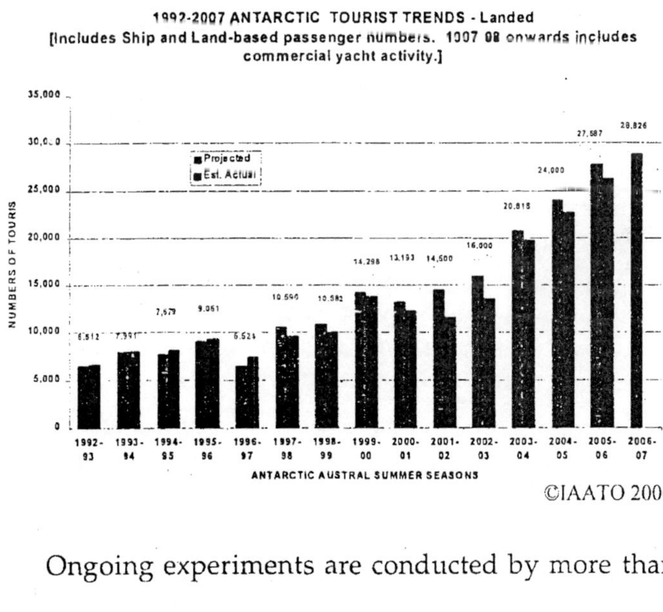

©IAATO 2006

Ongoing experiments are conducted by more than

4,000 scientists of many nationalities and with different research interests. Antarctica currently has no economic activity apart from offshore fishing and tourism, and these are run by other nations.

Antarctica is not an easy place to get to, but increasing numbers of people visit Antarctica every year. Almost all go as a part of an organized expeditionary cruise, frequently guided by experts who are a mixture of seasoned seafarers, and ice or wildlife experts. Tourism in the Antarctic is mainly by around 20 vessels carrying 45 to 280 passengers each. The ships are ice strengthened and sail primarily to the Antarctic Peninsula region. There have been occasional voyages to Antarctica by larger passenger vessels (up to 960 tourists), some of which conduct sightseeing cruises only without landings. Yacht travel is also very popular, and gives a more intimate contact, though often without the luxuries and facilities of the larger Antarctica cruise ship. Most trips take about 10 days to 3 weeks from port to port, though occasionally longer or shorter trips are possible. Peninsula voyages generally depart from Ushuaia in Argentina; other South American ports are occasionally used. The great majority of trips leave from South America; those that leave from elsewhere tend to be longer and more expensive. Hobart, Fremantle, Perth (Australia), Christchurch, Auckland, Littleton-Christchurch (New Zealand), Port Elizabeth, Cape Town (South Africa) are some of the other ports from where journeys begin.

No documentation or visas are required to visit Antarctica. However, the Antarctic Treaty framework and the presence of non-governmental travel organizations like the International Association of Antarctica Tour Operators (IAATO) play a crucial role in regulating tourist traffic and its impact to this continent of wonders.

outh America

South America

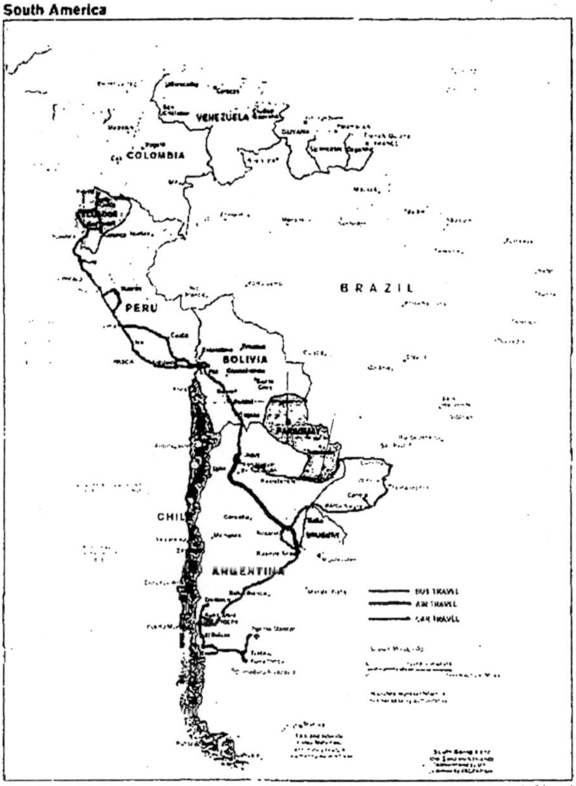

Few continents elicit such envy, and provoke such ıssionate pleas of "take me with you", as does South nerica. South America is a sub-continent crossed by e equator, with most of its area in the Southern emisphere. It consists of 12 countries and 3 major rritories and is in the southern hemisphere. It is nnected to North America by thin countries that make › Central America. It contains the massive Amazon River d surrounding basin—the largest tropical rain forest in the world; the toothy-edged Andes Mountains, that stretch the entire length of the continent, and some of the most diverse and spectacular landforms on the planet. Argentina, Bolivia, Brazil, Chile, Colombia, Ecuador, French Guiana, Guyana, Paraguay, Peru, Suriname, Uruguay, Venezuela, Falkland Islands (Islas Malvinas), and South Georgia and the South Sandwich Islands, are the South American countries and territories.

From the 1500s, the indigenous inhabitants of South America were invaded by European conquistadors; first from Spain and later from Portugal. The mixture of African, Indian and European influences have given South America a very distinct flavor. South America has a host of marvellous attractions, with most suitable for the whole family. One can find science, nature and history exhibits throughout the continent as well as a host of natural attractions, from volcanoes to cold glaciers and strange animals. The continent offers incredible pre-Columbian sights all along the Andes in Chile, Bolivia, Ecuador, Peru and Colombia. The best known of these are probably the Nazca Lines (Ica), Chan chan (trujillo) and Machu Picchu (cuzco) in Peru and Ciudad Perdida in Colombia. Any city has got it's own important archeological findings nearby. The Inca civilization didn't only leave archeological findings. From Colombia to Argentina, there language and culture is still alive. Furthermore in every South American country there are lots of stylish colonial churches and palaces.

If one is looking for an active holiday, there is good skiing in summer in Chile, Bolivia and Argentina; one can find the biggest rainforest and the longest river in the world in Brazil and there is great wildlife almost everywhere. The Wadden islands (off the coast of Ecuador) deserve a special mention here. The coast of

Venezuela and Colombia has great beaches and a very good atmosphere. Brazil has great beaches as well.

Those tourists who are into the fast paced life of big cities have a number of cities to choose from: Sao Paulo, Rio de Janeiro, Buenos Aires, Santiago or Lima all combine modern life with a south-American touch.

The Amazon River of South America is one of the longest two rivers on Earth, the Nile River in Africa being the other. The Amazon has by far the greatest total flow of any river, carrying more than the Mississippi, Nile, and Yangtze rivers combined. It also has the largest drainage area of any river system. The Amazon is responsible for a fifth of the total volume of fresh water entering the oceans worldwide. The Amazon rainforest in South America encompasses 1.2 billion acres with parts located within nine of the South American nations, with the he diversity of species in it the highest on earth. South America is home to many interesting species of animals including parrots, tarantulas, snakes, and mammals. The largest snake in the world, the Anaconda, lives in the rivers and dense forests of South America. Brightly colored poisonous frogs live inside the forests. The camel-like Llama is another important animal lives in South America.

The world's highest free-falling waterfall Angel Falls is located in the wilderness of Venezuela. Another important waterfall is Iguacu Falls, which is taller than Niagara Falls. The fact that the newly discovered Gocta Falls in Peru are the third largest in the world, says a lot about the exoticness of the South American continent. The world's second highest active volcano Cotopaxi (5897m) is situated about 50 km south of Quito, Ecuador.

Europe

No other region of the world approaches the popularity of Europe as a travel destination. Europe is neighbored by the Atlantic Ocean and Asia and is located in the northern hemisphere. Geographically, Europe is a subcontinent in the western portion of the larger continent known as Eurasia. The continent begins at the Ural Mountains in Russia, which define Europe's eastern boundary with Asia.

European culture has a broad influence beyond the continent of Europe due to the legacy of colonialism. The colonial legacy has spread European culture elsewhere in the world. Europe profoundly influenced on the cultures of Africa, India, Israel, Australia, and other places colonized or settled by Europeans. But what constitute European values is debatable: In recent decades the European Union has been seeking to identify and support common European values, however this has turned out to be a highly controversial issue. Most countries share common historical experiences, but several important divergences appear, the most notable being that between the East and the West. As a cultural and ethnic concept, the term Eastern Europe was defined by 19th century German nationalists to be synonymous with Slavic Europe, as opposed to Germanic (Western) Europe. The diversity on such a small territory in terms of language is proverbial. The European Union alone uses 21 official languages, which all have the same status. Russian is the most widely spoken domestic language in Europe, followed by German. Christianity is considered to be a dominant unifying feature in shaping a collective European culture for at least the last 1700 years. However, mutually dissecting denominations of Christians like the Catholics, the Protestants, and the Orthodox Christians all have their faiths as official faiths in certain countries in the continent. There are handful countries with significant Muslim population, too.

There are 45 countries in the Europe. The list of European countries is given below:

Albania	Andorra
Austria	Belarus
Belgium	Bosnia and Herzegovina
Bulgaria	Croatia
Cyprus	Czech Republic
Denmark	Estonia
Finland	France
Germany	Greece
Hungary	Iceland
Ireland	Italy

Latvia
Liechtenstein
Lithuania
Luxembourg
Macedonia
Malta
Moldova
Monaco
Netherlands
Norway
Poland
Portugal
Romania
Russia
San Marino
Serbia and Montenegro
Slovak Republic
Slovenia
Spain
Sweden
Switzerland
Turkey
Ukraine
United Kingdom

Vatican City Some of the most popular attractions available in the Europe are:

1. Eiffel Tower (Paris, France)
2. Big Ben (London, United Kingdom)
3. Buckingham Palace (London, United Kingdom)
4. Chateau de Versailles (Paris, France)
5. Parliament Building (Budapest, Hungary)
6. Westminster Abbey (London, United Kingdom)
7. Tower Bridge Exhibition (London, United Kingdom)
8. White House (Warsaw, Poland)
9. Colosseum (Rome, Italy)
10. Duomo (Milan, Italy)

The most popular European destinations are:

1. London
2. Amsterdam
3. Rome

4. Venice
5. Vienna
6. Zurich
7. Paris
8. Florence
9. Lucerne
10. Munich

North America

North America consists of 50 states and is in the northern hemisphere. It is bordered on the north by the Arctic Ocean, on the east by the North Atlantic Ocean, on the southeast by the Caribbean Sea, and on the south and west by the North Pacific Ocean; South America lies to the southeast. Geopolitically, Northern America is sometimes used to refer to USA, Canada, Greenland, and Bermuda. Sometimes, Mexico and Belize are also included in it even though the UN treats them as belonging to Central America.

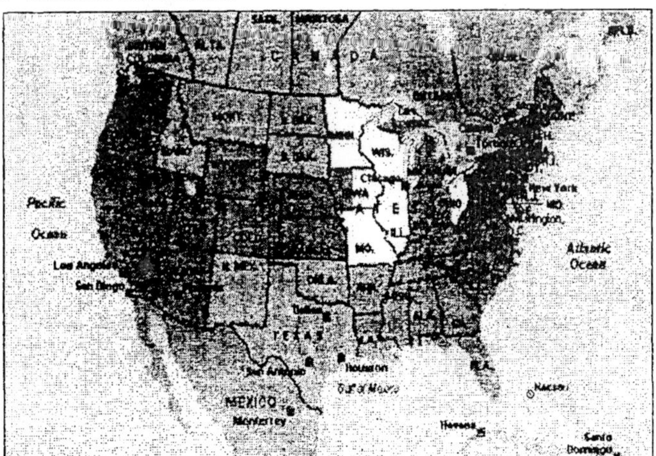

Socially and culturally, North America presents a wel defined entity. Canada and the United States have a shared culture and similar traditions as a result of both countries being former British colonies. A common cultural and economic market has been developed between the two nations because of the strong economic and historical ties. Spanish-speaking North America shares a common past as well. Central American and Spanish-speaking Caribbean nations have historically had more in common due to geographical proximity and the fact that, after winning independence from Spain, Mexico never took part in an effort to build a Central American Union.

Economically, Canada and the United States are the wealthiest and the most developed nations in the continent; the countries of Central America and the Caribbean much less developed, while Mexico lies between these two extremes.

The list of countries in North America is given below:

Antigua and Barbuda	The Bahamas
Barbados	Belize
Canada	Costa Rica
Cuba	Dominica
Dominican Republic	El Salvador
Greenland (Kalaallit Nunaat)	Grenada
Guatemala	Haiti
Honduras	Jamaica
Mexico	Nicaragua
Panama	Saint Kitts and Nevis
Saint Lucia	Saint Vincent and the Grenadines
Trinidad and Tobago	United States of America

Although the population of Canada and the United States is still largely of European origin, it is growing increasingly diverse with substantial immigration from Asia, Latin America, and Africa. North America's extensive agricultural lands (especially in Canada and the United States) are a result of the interrelationship of favorable climatic conditions, fertile soils, and technology. However, the manufacturing that provided a high standard of living for the people of Canada and the United States has significantly declined, and formerly abundant factory jobs are increasingly replaced by those in the service sector.

Because population centers are often widely spaced, most long-range travel is by air, with an extensive network of major hubs and smaller regional airports, usually supplemented with car rental services to cover local travel. Almost all highways in Canada and the United States are well maintained, with amenities such as gas, food, and lodging ranging from adequate to very convenient to excessive. Most travel in Canada, the United States, and Mexico is by personal vehicle. Whatever remaining part of train travel does not offer either speed, comfort, or convenience.

Asia

Asia, the largest continent, is traditionally defined as part of the landmass of Africa-Eurasia—with the western portion of the latter occupied by Europe—lying east of the Suez Canal, east of the Ural Mountains, and south of the Caucasus Mountains and the Caspian and Black Seas. It contains the major portion of the largest country in the world, Russia. Asia was the home of some of the world's oldest civilizations. The empires of Sumer, Babylonia, Assyria, Media, and Persia and the civilizations of Islam flourished in SW Asia, while in the east the ancient civilizations of India, China, and Japan prospered.

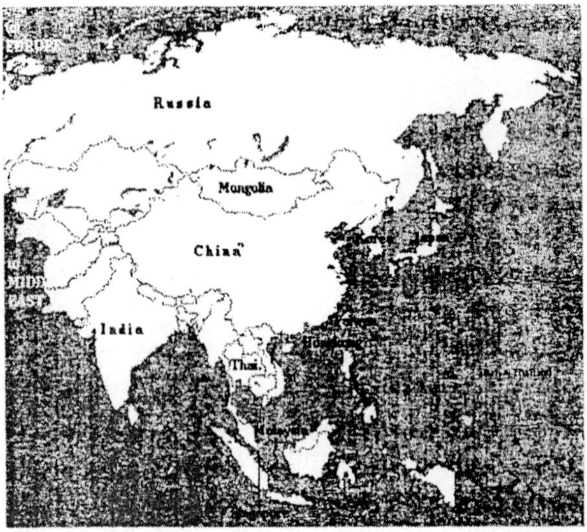

Asia can be divided into six regions, each possessing distinctive physical, cultural, economic, and political characteristics. Southwest Asia (Iran; Turkey, in Asia Minor; and the nations of the Fertile Crescent and the Arabian Peninsula or Arabia), long a strategic crossroad, is characterized by an arid climate and irrigated agriculture, great petroleum reserves, and the predominance of Islam. South Asia (Afghanistan and the nations of the Indian subcontinent) is isolated from the rest of Asia by great mountain barriers. Southeast Asia (the nations of the southeastern peninsula and the Malay Archipelago) is characterized by monsoon climate, maritime orientation, the fusion of Indian and Chinese cultures, and a great diversity of ethnic groups, languages, religions, and politics. East Asia (China, Mongolia, Korea, and the islands of Taiwan and Japan) is located in the mid-latitudes on the Pacific Ocean, and is characterized by cultures strongly influenced by civilizations of the Huang He and Chang (Yangtze) river systems. It forms the most industrialized region of Asia. Russian Asia (in the northern third of the continent) consists of the vast region of Siberia and the Russian Far East. In the center of the continent is Central Asia, formed of a set of independent former republics of the Soviet Union. This region is characterized by desert conditions and irrigated agriculture, with ancient traditions of nomadic herding.

The distribution of Asia's huge population is governed by climate and topography, with the monsoons and the fertile alluvial plains determining the areas of greatest density. Almost two thirds of Asia's indigenous population is of Mongolic stock. Major religions are Hinduism (in India); Theravada Buddhism (in Sri Lanka, Myanmar, Thailand, Cambodia, Vietnam, and Laos); Lamaism, or Tibetan Buddhism (in Mongolia and China, particularly Tibet); East Asian Buddhism (in China and Korea, mixed with Confucianism, shamanism, and Taoism; in Japan mixed with Shinto and Confucianism); Islam (in SW and S Asia, W central Asia, and Indonesia); and Catholicism (in the Philippines, East Timor, and Vietnam).

The list of countries in Asia is given below:

Afghanistan	Bahrain
Bangladesh	Bhutan
Brunei	Cambodia
China	Cyprus
East Timor	India
Indonesia	Iran
Iraq	Israel
Japan	Jordan
Kazakhstan	Kuwait
Kyrgyzstan	Laos

Lebanon
Malaysia
Maldives
Mongolia
Myanmar
Nepal
North Korea
Oman
Pakistan
Philippines
Qatar
Russia
Saudi Arabia
Singapore
South Korea
Sri Lanka
Syria
Taiwan
Tajikistan
Thailand
Turkey
Turkmenistan
United Arab Emirates
Uzbekistan
Vietnam
Yemen

Some of the highly visited destinations in Asia are:

Cebu, Philippines
Langkawi Malaysia
Phuket, Thailand
Manila, Philippines
Kuala Lumpur, Malaysia
Bali, Indonesia
Hong Kong
Ko Chang Islands, Thailand
Chiang Mai, Chiang Rai Thailand
Bangkok, Thailand
Ko Samui Islands, Thailand
Penang, Malaysia
Singapore
Hawaii
Kerala, India
Tokyo, Japan
Shanghai, China
Seoul, South Korea
Taipei, Taiwan
Beijing, China
Macau
Guam
Taj Mahal, India
Pacific Islands

Australia and New Zealand

Australia and New Zealand comes under the larger macro-geographical formation, namely Oceania. The name Oceania is used because unlike the other continental

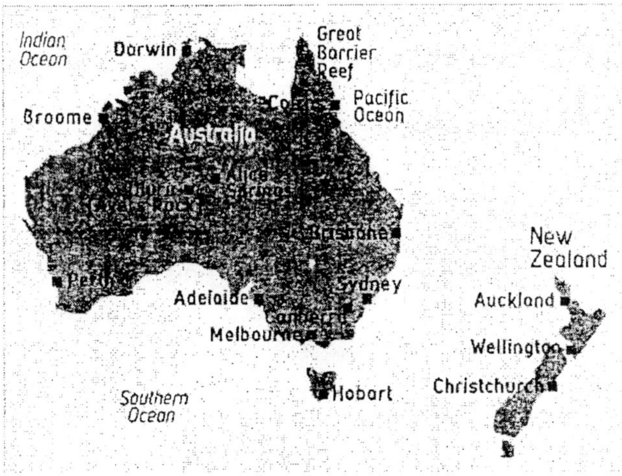

roupings, it is the ocean and adjacent seas rather than continent that link the lands together. The exact scope f Oceania is defined variously, with interpretations icluding Australia, New Zealand, New Guinea, and arious islands of the Malay Archipelago. Oceania has een traditionally divided into Micronesia, Melanesia, olynesia, and Australasia. Australasia is the major-most ortion and is made up of Australia, New Zealand, Norfolk land, Cocos Islands, and Christmas Island and is by far e largest region in Oceania. Micronesia includes the aroline Islands, Marshall Islands, and Mariana Islands. elanesia includes New Guinea, the Admiralty Islands, e Bismarck and Louisiade archipelagoes, the Solomon lands, the Santa Cruz Islands, New Caledonia and the oyalty Islands, Vanuatu, Fiji, Norfolk Island, and imerous others. The principal groups in Polynesia are e Hawaiian Islands, Samoa, Tonga, and the islands of ench Polynesia. Ethnologically though not ographically, Polynesia embraces New Zealand.

Australia

Australia is located in the South East of Asia in the south Pacific. This continent is over 2,000 miles across. It's about the same size as the 48 mainland states of the USA and 50 per cent larger than Europe, but has the lowest population density in the world - only two people per square kilometer.

Australia has a prosperous, Western-style mixed economy, and was ranked third in the United Nations 2005 Human Development Index. The service sector of the economy, including tourism, education, and financial services, comprises more than two third of GDP.

The kangaroo is unique to Australia and one of our most easily recognized mammals. There are more kangaroos in Australia now than when Australia was first settled. Estimates suggest around 40 million. The Great Barrier Reef, the world's largest coral reef, lies a short distance off the north-east coast and extends for over 2,000 kilometers. The world's largest monolith, Mount Augustus, is located in Western Australia. Coober Pedy in South Australia is known as the opal capital of the world. Australia's 101 million sheep (mostly merinos), found on around 53,000 properties, produce more than 70 per cent of the world's wool. With 27 million head of cattle, Australia is the world's largest exporter of beef. Australia supports at least 25,000 species of plants, while Europe only supports 17,500. Australia has so many outstanding places to visit during a vacation that it is difficult to choose among them. Popular regions for tourists are: Queensland, Victoria, Northern Territory, Tasmania, New South Wales, Australian Capital Territory, South Australia, and Western Australia. Some of the notable attractions in Australia are:

The Great Barrier Reef: This is Australia's number one attraction. Over 1,400 miles in length, the Great Barrier Reef is billed as the world's largest natural feature. Consisting of thousands of individual reefs and over 600 islands, the Great Barrier Reef is best enjoyed if you dive or scuba.

The Red Center: It is located in the Northern Territory, is both the physical and spiritual center of Australia. This is the site of the world famous Uluru (Ayers Rock), a reddish rock that is the world's largest monolith. Posing in stark contrast to its flat surrounding, Uluru is best viewed at sunrise and sunset when its color seems to change in mysterious and magical ways.

Sydney: It has got many attractions and a great setting in which to enjoy them. The city's harbor features the spectacular Opera House, the Rocks (the original penal colony in Australia), Darling Harbor, and the Sydney Harbor Bridge.

Melbourne: It is considered by many to be the most stylish of Australian cities. The City's mix of modern and Victorian architectures blends in an attractive manner.

Adelaide: It is the entry point for an exploration of South Australia. The area is, also, the home to many of Australia's best vineyards.

New Zealand

Although New Zealand is far indeed in absolute terms from Australia, many persist in confusing the two countries. The similarities between the two countries are a lot. The great Polynesian navigator Kupe first found his way here around 1000AD, and then Captain Cook's arrival in 1769 unleashed a sea of change for the land and its inhabitants.

New Zealand is in the Southern Temperate Zone: the climate is fairly mild, without the extremes experienced in many other countries. However, New Zealand has a cooler climate since it lies closer to Antarctica, which gives rise to a landscape, that both varied and scenic. The languages spoken are English and Maori. The ethnic composition is: European (88%); Maori (9 %); and, Pacific Islander and Others (2 %). New Zealand has a special relationship with some island countries of the South Pacific, the Cook Islands, Niue and Tokelau.

New Zealand is noted as one of the best activity-oriented tourist destinations in the world. Many backpackers visit it to get involved in activities, ranging from skiing, snowboarding, bungee jumping and skydiving to white water rafting. An extremely popular activity is tramping or hiking. This is the best way to explore the wilderness of New Zealand and walks can range from one hour long to five days long. Many backpackers take the opportunity to do a glacier hike whilst in New Zealand too.

Islands are scattered all around the edges of New Zealand's coastline. Some are no bigger than a tennis court; others are the size of a small country. They are hideaways for rare bird species or escape hatches for city dwellers. Many are protected from development or habitation, so that they can be enjoyed in their most natural state.

The Kiwi, for which New Zealand is mostly known, lives only in New Zealand. Although primarily a bird of New Zealand's native forests, kiwis also live in scrub and native grasslands.

The major tourist regions in New Zealand are: Auckland, Christchurch, Wellington, and Queenstown.

International Air Transport Association Regions

International Air Transport Association (IATA) Traffic Conference (TC) areas and sub-areas are geographical areas recognized and indicated in the Passenger Air Tariff. Some other important terms in the IATA geography are:

Gateway City refers to the main port of arrival into a country.

Attraction refers to a discrete destination, comprising natural and/or constructed features, which draws visitors and/or tourists to it.

Features, in the context of this unit standard, may include but are not limited to - opening hours, price range, location, what there is to see and do, duration, and time of year.

Elapsed Transportation Time is the actual time it takes to travel from one place to another.

Journey refers to travel between two or more points.

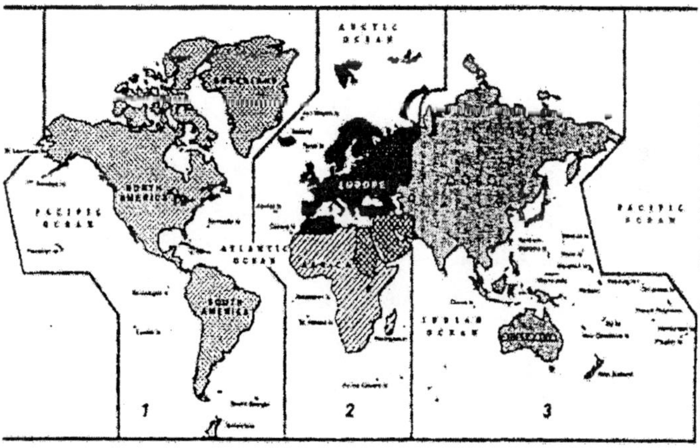

AREA 1
Comprises what is called the "Western Hemisphere"

AREAS 2 and 3
Comprise what is called the "Eastern Hemisphere"

The Travel Conference Areas are listed below:

TC1 Mexico sub-area

TC1 Caribbean sub-area

TC1 Longhaul sub-area

TC1 Within South America sub-area

TC2 Within Europe sub-area

TC2 Within Middle East sub-area

TC2 Within Africa sub-area

TC2 Europe-Middle East sub-area

TC2 Europe-Africa sub-area

TC2 Middle East-Africa sub-area

TC3 South Asian Subcontinent sub-area

TC3 South East Asia sub-area

TC3 South West Pacific sub-area

TC3 Japan/Korea sub-area

TC3 South Asian Subcontinent-South East Asia sub-area

TC3 South Asian Subcontinent-South West Pacific sub-area

TC3 South Asian Subcontinent-Japan/Korea sub-area

TC3 South East Asia-South West Pacific sub-area

TC3 South East Asia-Japan/Korea sub-area

TC3 South West Pacific-Japan/Korea sub-area

TC12 North Atlantic-Europe sub-area

TC12 North Atlantic-Middle East sub-area

TC12 North Atlantic-Africa sub-area

TC12 Mid Atlantic-Europe sub-area

TC12 Mid Atlantic-Middle East sub-area

TC12 Mid Atlantic-Africa sub-area

TC12 South Atlantic-Europe sub-area

TC12 South Atlantic-Middle East sub-area

TC12 South Atlantic-Africa sub-area

TC123 (via TC2) North Atlantic-South Asian Subcontinent sub-area

TC123 (via TC2) North Atlantic-South East Asia sub-area

TC123 (via TC2) North Atlantic-Japan/Korea sub-area

TC123 (via TC2) North Atlantic-South West Pacific sub-area

TC123 (via TC2) Mid Atlantic-South Asian Subcontinent sub-area

TC123 (via TC2) Mid Atlantic-South East Asia sub-area

TC123 (via TC2) Mid Atlantic-Japan/Korea sub-area

TC123 (via TC2) Mid Atlantic-South West Pacific sub-area

TC123 (via TC2) South Atlantic-South Asian Subcontinent sub-area

TC123 (via TC2) South Atlantic-South East Asia sub-area

TC123 (via TC2) South Atlantic-Japan/Korea sub-area

TC123 (via TC2) South Atlantic-South West Pacific sub-area

TC23/TC123 (via TC1) Europe-South Asian Subcontinent sub-area

TC23/TC123 (via TC1) Europe-South East Asia sub-area

TC23/TC123 (via TC1) Europe-South West Pacific sub-area

TC23/TC123 (via TC1) Europe-Japan/Korea sub-area

TC23/TC123 (via TC1) Middle East-South Asian Subcontinent sub-area

TC23/TC123 (via TC1) Middle East-South East Asia sub-area

TC23/TC123 (via TC1) Middle East-South West Pacific sub-area

TC23/TC123 (via TC1) Middle East-Japan/Korea sub-area

TC23/TC123 (via TC1) Africa-South Asian Subcontinent sub-area

TC23/TC123 (via TC1) Africa-South East Asia sub-area

TC23/TC123 (via TC1) Africa-South West Pacific sub-area

TC23/TC123 (via TC1) Africa-Japan/Korea sub-area

TC31 North and Central Pacific-South Asian Subcontinent sub-area

TC31 North and Central Pacific-South East Asia sub-area

TC31 North and Central Pacific-Japan/Korea sub-area

TC31 South Pacific sub-area

Important Tourist Destinations in India

India has a very rich and dynamic culture that attracts every traveler. A living museum waiting to be explored, felt and cherished - India presents a vast canvas in vivid and myriad shades of passionate hues. India is a spiritual land, a land where the religion and philosophy have attained their cultivating points. Much like its food, Indian culture is rich and diverse. With rivers, seas, mountains and deserts, India is a vast subcontinent bringing together people of different languages and numerous dialects. In each region people embrace their own languages and beliefs, making India a land full of history and tradition. India has tremendous variations in topography and climate from the desert regions of Rajasthan to the scenic hill stations, green valleys of Himachal Pradesh, the rain forests of the North East, the extensive sun-drenched beaches, the wild sanctuaries.

For the sake of convenience, we divide tourism in India to tourism in four broad geographical segments:

Tourism in East and North East India

Orissa: Bhubaneswar-the state capital of Orissa with its over a hundred temples-provides an ideal introduction to the East India. Visits to the Lingaraja Temple and the Rajarani Temple are a must. One of the four religious centers in India, Puri in Orissa is famous for its Jagannath Temple. Other temples of interest here are the Gundicha, Lokanath and Tota Gopinath and tanks like Śweta Ganga and indradyumna. With its famous Sun Temple, Konark is the high point of a visit to the Golden Triangle of Orissa. The temple, built in the 13th century is replete with stone sculptures.

State tourism website: www.orissatourism.gov.in

West Bengal: West Bengal is also one of the first destinations in a tourist's itinerary visiting the eastern part of the country. Calcutta (also Kolkata), the capital of the state, is the proud intellectual capital of the country. The Victoria Memorial is a grand edifice constructed in the memory of Queen Victoria. Howrah Bridge is another landmark that denotes the city of joy. Shantiniketan, Tagore's university township, is a must on any itinerary that plots Bengal as a stopover. For witnessing the sheer magnificence of mountains, unsullied and pristine, one should visit the hill station of Darjeeling, located 7,000 feet above sea level. One can also undertake short trips to Mirik, land of oranges, and the charming city of Kalimpong, famous for its orchids and curio shops. The Jaldapara Wildlife Sanctuary is known for elephants and other wild animals. Besides these, West Bengal has lot more to offer as a tourist destination. Digha, Siliguri, Gaur, Pandua, Murshidabad, Bishnupur, Haldia and the Sunderban Tiger Reserve are some of the few places of West Bengal that need to be mentioned here.

State tourism website: www.wbtourism.com

Bihar: Patna in Bihar is a city abounding in the relics of the bygone ages. Takht Harmandir Saheb is of religious importance to the Sikhs and is believed to be the place of birth of the last Sikh guru, Govind Singh. Thirty kilometers from Patna is Maner, a medieval stronghold of the Turks and the site of the shrines of Hazrat Makhdum Yahya Maneri and his son Shafruddin Ahmed Maneri. The remains of an ancient fort with massive cyclopean walls together with other sites amidst lush green surroundings of Rajgriha recreate the glory of the past. Nalanda, in the heart of Bihar, stands as the world's most ancient seat of learning. The ruins confirm the university's ability to cater to the needs of 10,000 students until the 12th century AD. Bodh Gaya houses the site of the sacred Mahabodhi tree where the Buddha attained enlightenment. Rajmahal is a medieval settlement on the eastern fringe of Bihar. It is believed to have been founded by Raja Man Singh, the Rajput general of Emperor Akbar. Then there is the Hazaribagh Wildlife Sanctuary nestling at a low terrain (1,800 feet). Hazaribagh is also vying for a place in the international heritage list for its recent findings of rock paintings, caves, stone age tools and smelted iron slag that shows a much early advent of the Iron Age than the theorized Chalcolithic age.

State tourism website: http://bstdc.bih.nic.in

Assam: In Guwahati in Assam, it is customary for anyone on his first visit to this city to visit the Kamakhya temple, dedicated to the Mother Goddess. The importance of the temple is second only to the mighty Brahmaputra, the river with an undeniable presence in the town. The mighty Ahoms reigned supreme for 600 years at Sibsagar, at a distance of 369 km from Guwahati, where the ruins of their temples and palaces still exist. Resurrected by the Archeological Survey of India, these ruins provide an interesting insight into the past glory and splendor of Assam. Kaziranga National Park, situated at a distance of 217 km from Guwahati, is one of the most picturesque wildlife parks in India. Manas National Park (176 km from Guwahati), situated amidst the gentle slopes of the Himalayas, is the only tiger reserve of its kind in the entire region. Pabitora, a small wildlife sanctuary, 60 km from Guwahati is also worth a visit. Rhino and various species of deer abound here.

Hajo, 32 km west of Guwahati, is a sacred place for Hindus, Muslims, and Buddhists.

State tourism website: www.assamtourism.org

Sikkim: In Sikkim, one can visit Changthang (the origin of the river Teesta), Yumthang (140 km from Gangtok), the Singba Rhododendron Sanctuary (137 km from Gangtok), and the Kanchanjunga National Park. South Sikkim is famous for trekking and offers some of the best treks in the region. One can walk through the sylvan mountains of Namtse, 100 km from Gangtok, and Tendong hill, Varsey, Borong, Maenam hill, and Ravangla. In the eastern part of the state, one can visit the capital Gangtok with its numerous attractions. West Sikkim boasts of the Rabdentse ruins, Pelling, and the former capital Yuksom.

State tourism website: www.sikkiminfo.net/travel_guide.htm

Arunachal Pradesh: Arunachal provides a host of sites of tourist interest. Its capital at Itanagar tells the story of the Ita Fort built in the fourteenth century by King Ramchandra of Mayapur. Mallini Than is another unique site that goes back to the 10th and 12th century. It has an ancient temple housing sculptures of gods and goddesses of the Hindu iconographic school. Parasuram Kund and the Brahma Kund in the Lohit district are sacred places that attract thousands of pilgrims to take a dip in their holy waters and purge themselves of their sins. Bismaknagar and its fort in the Dibang valley are memorials to the Bhagwat Gita, story of Lord Krishna's visit there and his elopement with a local girl, Rukmini.The Tawang Monastery, constructed in the 17th century, houses a big library of holy books, some of which are written in gold letters.

State tourism website: www.arunachaltourism.com

Nagaland: Nagaland is situated on the easternmost region of India. One of the seven sister states India, Nagaland is covered mostly by high-altitude mountains. The hospitability of the people here and their culture and tradition simply touch the heart. Moreover, the Nagaland is an ideal destination for trekking, rock climbing and jungle camping.

State tourism website: http://nagaland.nic.in/potential/tourism.htm

Tripura: The state of Tripura has several places of tourist importance like Agartala, Unakoti, Pilak, Udaipur, Tripurasundari Temple, Ujjayanta Palace, Neermahal, Jampui Hill, Bhavaneswari Temple, Sepahijala, Kamalasagar, Deotamura, and Dumboor Lake. Moreover, there are the Buddhist monasteries in Agartala, Pecharthal, Kanchanpur, Manu Bakul, Pilak, and Boxnagar.

State tourism website: http://tripura.nic.in

Manipur: Manipur has a lot to offer to the tourists visiting this state. Some of the places worth visiting are the Shree Govindajee Temple (a pilgrimage as well as historic center of the Vaishnavite), Kaina (a sacred place of Hindus), Khwairamand Bazaar (a market place run by women), Manipur Zoological Garden (renowned for the rare sangai deer), apart from the beautiful Loktak Lake and Sendra Island. Besides, Langthabal (historic sites), Moirang, Moreh, Phubala, Singda, Khongjom, Sahid Mandir, Khonghampat Orchidarium, Keibul Lamjao National Park, Sekta Archeological Living Museum, and the Manipur State Museum are surely worth a visit.

State tourism website: http://manipur.nic.in

Mizoram: Mizoram has many picturesque sites to visit. The Museum and Mini Zoological Garden at Aizawl, Bung (picnic spot), and Paikhai are worth a visit. Besides, the Tamdil natural lake (located 60 km away from Aizawl), Vantawng falls (137 km) and Champai (204 km) are some other picnic sites of the state.

State tourism website: http://mizotourism.nic.in

Meghalaya: Shillong is the capital of Meghalaya and the largest city. Shillong is the place to enjoy everything, starting from events, sightseeing, recreation, shopping, or unwinding oneself in a bar. Cherrapunji (58 km from Shillong), about two hours south of Shillong, used to the wettest place on earth. This honor is given today to Mausynram, a stone throw further west. The area is lush green with waterfalls and an extensive underground cave network. A popular picnic spot is the Mawjinbuim Cave (55 km off Shillong) where there is a stalagmite in the form of a Shiva lingam receiving steady drops of water from a stone formed like a breast. Jowai, is the gateway to Nartiang, a delightful village further north that has a bizarre collection of druid stones. Other places to visit are Jakrem (66 km from Shillong), which is famous for its hot springs. Nawphlang is a picnic spot, and Ranigodam is known for adventure sports like angling. The untouched 220-sq-km Balpakram National Park south of Tura features the canyon of the Mahadeo River, with fauna including tigers.

State tourism website: www.meghalayatourism.com

Tourism in West India

The states of Gujarat, Maharashtra, Daman & Diu, and

Goa are generally considered as the western part of India and are the most economically developed region of the country. One common thread that binds all the states is the Arabian Sea, whose shores are shared by all.

Gujarat: Gujarat is dotted with several places to visit and see. Amongst the popular tourist destinations of Gujarat are Ahmedabad, Gandhinagar, Jamnagar, Patan, Vadodara, Pavagadh, Champaner, Surat, Saputara, Rajkot, Bhavnagar, Junagadh, Uperkot, Porbandar, Kutch and Bhuj.

State tourism website: www.gujarattourism.com

Maharashtra: Opening some of the most enduring chapters of Indian civilization, Maharashtra offers a wide range of tourist attractions to choose from. Starting from Mumbai, the largest metropolis in India and also its financial capital to Ajanta and Ellora to Mahabaleshwar to Pune to Aurangabad to Lonavala, the state of Maharashtra makes its impression on the mind and soul of the visitors strongly.

State tourism website: *www.maharashtratourism.gov.in*

Goa: Goa is best known for its beautiful beaches, forts, churches, waterfalls, seminaries, and caves. Some of the fine beaches in Goa are Anjuna, Calangute, Colva and Benaulim, Dona Paula, Vagator and Chapora, and others. The strong Roman Catholic community, with the active support of the erstwhile Portuguese rulers, has had a number of churches built in this picturesque locale. Some of the well known churches in Goa are Lady of Immaculate Conception and the Chapel of St. Sebastian, Se Catedral, Basilica of Bom Jesus, Convent and Church of St. Francis of Assisi, Church of St. Cajetan, Church of St. Augustine Ruins, Church and Convent of St. Monica, Church of Our Lady of Rosary, Chapel of St.

Anthony and Chapel of St. Catherine-all of which are in Old Goa.

State tourism website: www.goatourism.org

Daman & Diu: In Daman, one can visit the Fort of St. Jerome at Nani Daman, where there is a Jain temple as well. The stately Light House, the amusement park and the Gandhi Park at Daman jetty are also places of interest. Among the beaches, Devka beach is the most famous. The lake garden of Satya Nagar Udyan is famous for its fountains and promenades. In Diu, the Zampa Gateway is of particular interest. It has carvings of lions, angels and a priest and has a chapel inside with an inscription dating back to 1702. The artificial Zampa waterfall is also attractive.

State tourism website: www.damantourism.com

Tourism in North India

The North Indian Plains consist of the Indus basin, the Ganga-Brahmaputra basin, and the tributaries of these mighty river systems. The northern Indian region saw one of the earliest civilizations on earth, the Harappan or Indus Civilization. From than onwards, this region remained in the center of many great moments of human civilization. Coming of Aryans; Vedic Age; the age of Great Epics; formation of Mahajanpadas; rise and fall of great empires like Mauryas, Guptas, Delhi Sultanate, and Mughals; and at the end of it all the oppressive British, and the freedom of India in 1947. This region has seen all this and more. Like it saw the emergence of some of the greatest religions on earth, like Buddhism, Hinduism, Jainism, and Sikhism. Great spiritual minds and great religions created an amazing land that had space for everyone.

The North of India consists of Uttar Pradesh, Himachal Pradesh, Jammu & Kashmir, Uttaranchal, Punjab, Haryana, Rajasthan, Madhya Pradesh and Chattisgarh.

Uttar Pradesh: The Taj at Agra is, of course, the best place to start with. This superb specimen of Mughal architecture is a veritable poetry in stone constructed by Shahjahan in memory of his wife Mumtaz. Located 40 km away is Fatehpur Sikri built by Akbar. Almora is a visitor's delight. There is the temple of Kaushik Devi on the Kashyap Hill. According to the Puranas, Kaushik Devi appeared from the body of Goddess Parvati to kill the demons Shumbh-Nishumbh. The Corbett National Park, situated in a region between the Himalayan and Shivalik ranges on both the banks of Ramganga in northern Uttar Pradesh, is renowned all over the world for its scenic beauty and wildlife. It is a prominent center of attraction for Indian and foreign tourists alike. It has the distinction of being the first national park in India.

State tourism website: www.up-tourism.com

Himachal Pradesh: Located in the charming Kullu valley in Himachal Pradesh and set amongst the lower reaches of the mighty Himalayas, the small town of Kullu is famous for its temples, apple orchards, and the annual Dussehra festival, all of which attract hordes of tourists. One of the most beautiful hill stations of the country, Manali is basically a small town in the Kullu valley of Himachal Pradesh. Termed sometimes as the cradle between the lesser Himalayas, Manali is extremely popular with tourists for its lavish display of unspoilt natural beauty. Rich in its scenic splendor, Manali draws a good number of tourists from within the country and abroad every year. There are several other tourist sites in the North Indian state of Himachal Pradesh

State tourism website: http://himachaltourism.nic.in

Jammu & Kashmir: Srinagar, the state capital, is the most famous tourist destination in the state. An ancient city, there are many attractions that can attract even the most unwilling of tourists to this magical land. Dal Lake, Nishat Bagh, Shalimar Bagh, and Chashme Shahi are some of the best-known tourist spot in Srinagar. Jammu is the winter capital of the state and next in importance after Srinagar. Most of the tourists who come to the Jammu region have the Mata Vaishno Devi shrine as their destination, which is quite close by. However, the spirit of holiness permeates through the entire city, so much so that Jammu is also known as the City of Temples. The other major tourist attraction is the Raghunath Temple Complex, which is the largest temple in North India devoted to Lord Rama.

State tourism website: www.jktourism.org

Uttaranchal: The major destinations are Haridwar, Rishikesh, Dehradun, Mussoorie, Almora, Kedarnath, Badrinath, Yamunotri, Gangotri, Jim Corbett National Park, Nainital, Ranikhet, and Pithoragarh. High- and low-altitude trekking, river rafting, para gliding, hang-gliding, mountaineering, skiing, etc are some of the recreational opportunities available at Uttaranchal.

State tourism website: *www.ua.nic.in/uttaranchaltourism*

Punjab: The most important tourist center in the state is Amritsar with its Golden Temple. This temple is considered to be the holiest of all the pilgrimages of Sikhism and houses Akal Takht, the supreme governing body of Sikhism. Wagah is the only open land point between India and Pakistan. The Changing of Guards and the ceremonial lowering of the flags ceremony at sundown are great tourist attractions and have their own symbolic importance. Ludhiana is famous for its hosiery and woolen goods and products from Ludhiana are exported all over the world. Patiala is famous for its healthy food, loving people, wonderful parandaas, exciting Patiala peg and jootis. The capital city of Chandigarh is considered to be a Mecca of modern architecture and planning all over the world.

State tourism website: www.punjabtourism.org

Haryana: Surajkund with its large sun pool and amphitheatre, combines proximity to the national capital with many amenities and comforts in an ambience that is typically rural and far away from the trappings of the urban centres. Haryana is proud of its many lake retreats besides Badkhal and Karna. There is the Tilyar Lake at Rohtak, 70 kilometres away from Delhi, with facilities like boating and kayaking. In a different direction and located 64 kilometres from Delhi on the old highway to Alwar, is the Damdama Lake with cottages built on higher ground and mirrored in the calm waters of the lake. Haryana is proud of its many lake retreats besides Badkhal and Karna. There is the Tilyar Lake at Rohtak, 70 kilometres away from Delhi, with facilities like boating and kayaking. In a different direction and located 64 kilometres from Delhi on the old highway to Alwar, is the Damdama Lake with cottages built on higher ground and mirrored in the calm waters of the lake.

State tourism website: http://haryanatourism.com

Rajasthan: Rajasthan's almost 80% of the places are regarded as the places of tourist interest. The old city of Jaipur, capital to the state of Rajasthan, painted pink that gives a magical glow to the city, is one of the must visit places of the state. The 250-year-old city of Jaipur, also known popularly as the Pink City is a startling blend of forts and palaces, teeming markets and all the bustle and modernity befitting the capital of India's second largest State. The Hawa Mahal, the exquisite City Palace and the incredible observatory of Maharaja Sawai Jai Singh II Central Museum, Nagar Garh Fort, Jaigarh Fort, Amber, Albert Museum, Birla Mandir Planetarium, Sisodia Rani Park, Lakshmi Narain Temple, Kanak Vrindavan, The Rajmahal Palace, Rambagh Palace (now a Luxury hotel) and the Jantar Mantar are some of the sites that say about their contemporary time. There are several other tourist attractions in the North Indian state of Rajasthan.

State tourism website: www.rajasthantourism.gov.in

Chattisgarh: It has been formed on November 1, 2000, as India's 26th state. It has major tourist centres like Amarkantak, Banjari Baba, Bhoramdev, Champaranya, Chitrakoot, Dudhadharimath, Indrawati National Park, Kangerghati National Park, Jagdalpur, Bastar, Danteswari Temple, etc. Korba is a center of production of *Kosa* , a lightweight fabric with a sheen that makes it a favorite for making casual garments as well as club wear. Major cities are Raipur, Durg-Bhilai (twin cities), Bilaspur, Rajnandgaon, Korba, Raigarh and Jagdalpur.

State tourism website: www.chhattisgarhtourism.net

Tourism in South India

To the south of the Great Plains of northern India lie the Great Plateau of Peninsular India, which is divided into two parts, namely, the Malwa Plateau and the Deccan Plateau. The Malwa plateau bounded by the Aravali hills in the northwest and the Vindhyas in the south form the northern half of this peninsula. The valley of the Narmada

River forms the southern boundary of this plateau. The Deccan plateau extends from the Satpura hills in the north to Kanyakumari, the southernmost tip of mainland India, finally ending in the Indian Ocean.

Tamil Nadu: Chennai, the capital city, offers some beautiful beach resorts. The best place to start a temple tour is Mamallapuram, a seaside village that, apart from some exquisite Pallava rock-cut architecture, boasts a long stretch of sun-kissed beach. Inland, the pilgrimage city of Kanchipuram is filled with reminders of an illustrious past under successive dynastic rulers, while further down the coast is one of India's rare French colonial possessions, Pondicherry, where Auroville has found a new role in the 'New Age'. The road south from Pondicherry puts one back on the temple trail, leading to the Chola kingdom and the extraordinary architecture of Chidambaram, Gangaikondacholapuram, Kumbhakonam and Darasuram. For the best Chola bronzes and a glimpse of the magnificent paintings that flourished under Maratha rajas in the eighteenth century, travelers should head for Thanjavur. The city boasts of almost a hundred temples and was the birthplace of the Bharatnatyam dance. Tamil Nadu's temples are undeniably its major attraction, it would take months to see them all, and there is plenty else to distract even the most ardent architecture buff. In the west of the state, where the hill stations of Kodaikanal and Ooty are the premier attractions, sylvan hills offer mountain views and a network of trails winds through forests and tea and coffee plantations.

State tourism website: www.tamilnadutourism.org

Kerala: The entire state of Kerala is a tourist destination and at every corner of this state, one can experience something new. It is not without any reason that the Keralites call their state the 'God's Own Country'. Backwaters, historical structures, culture, wildlife, and natural beauty, the state has all these and more.The major tourist destinations in the state include Thiruvananthapuram, Kochi, Kovalam, Thrissur, Kozhikode, Munnar, Palakkad, Alappuzha, Kollam, Kannur, Periyar Wildlife Sanctuary, and Sabrimalai etc. The state has given great emphasis on eco tourism and new experiments are being done to take tourism nearer to the general public. In this way too, the state is a pioneer in the country.

State tourism website: www.keralatourism.org

Andhra Pradesh: Hyderabad the capital of Andhra Pradesh has several prominent places in and around it. It has a Hindu-Muslim culture with a number of monuments of historical importance like Char Minar, Golconda, Salar Jung Museum, Mecca Masjid, Osman Sagar and Osmania University. The capital is in reality the twin cities of Hyderabad and Secunderabad linked together by the Hussain Sagar Lake. The other sites of historical importance in Andhra Pradesh include Warangal, Palampet, Vemulavada, Bhadrachalam, and Lepakshi. Andhra Pradesh is known for pilgrimages, not only for Hindus, but also for followers of other religions like Muslims, Christians and Buddhists. There are waterfalls at Ettipothala, Kuntala, and Gandipet. The caves at Undavalli and Borra are also major tourist attractions. Two large and world famous dams are located at Nagarjunasagar and Nizamsagar.

State tourism website: www.aptourism.com

Karnataka: Bangalore is the capital city and is also known as the Garden City because of its many beautiful gardens and parks. Now, due to the high concentration of IT industry, it also called the Silicon Valley of India. Hampi is famous for its ruins belonging to the erstwhile medieval Hindu kingdom of Vijayanagar and it has been declared a World Heritage site. The temples of Hampi, its monolithic sculptures and monuments, attract the traveler because of their excellent workmanship. The birthplace of the River Cauvery and home of some of India's bravest soldiers, Kodagu or Coorg, is noted for its scenic beauty. Mysore is the former capital of Karnataka. A city of palaces, people and smells, the princely city of Mysore is worth a visit whatever the month or season.

State tourism website: www.karnatakatourism.com

The South Indian Islands (Lakshadweep, Andaman and Nicobar): The white beaches, the lagoons that wash its shores with the coral reefs, which enclose it, and finally the deep blue sea, beckon tourists to the Lakshadweep islands in Southern India. Similarly, the Andaman and Nicobar Islands have Palm leaves dancing in the mild breeze, powder white beaches, the sound of waves breaking on a coral reef, lush, green rain forests and chirping rare birds.

State tourism website: http://tourism.andaman.nic.in

http://lakshadweeptourism.nic.in

On a very short list, India presents a mesmerizing collection of pulsating mega-sized metropolises, colorful towns and villages, stunning beaches, countless fairs and festivals, forts, lakes, monasteries, monuments, mosques, museums, palaces, shopping bazaars, temples, wildlife parks, many UNESCO World Heritage sites, and of course, an infinite variety of cultures and people.

In a place so varied and so interesting, it's difficult

to provide a brief list of things to see and do. However, not to be missed are the Taj Mahal, one of the premier destinations on the planet; nearby Agra Fort; Delhi, and the charms of both the old and new mixing together; the beaches and churches of Goa, and the beautiful Himalayan region.

India: Climate and Seasons

India is as large as a continent with a varying climate. Due to the country's great geographic size and varied topography, climate varies from one part of the country to the other. Many regions have their own microclimates, and the mean climatic conditions in Kashmir are very different from those in Kanyakumari in the extreme south.

India is in both the eastern and northern hemispheres. It is positioned on the Indian subcontinent in south-central Asia. It is bordered by the Arabian Sea, Bay of Bengal, Gulf of Mannar, Indian Ocean, and the countries of Pakistan, Afghanistan, China, Nepal, Bhutan, Bangladesh and Myanmar.

India's climate is strongly influenced by The Himalaya and the Thar Desert. The Himalaya ensure, by acting as a barrier to the cold north winds from Central Asia, that northern India is warm or mildly cool during winter and hot during summer. So, although the Tropic of Cancer passes almost through the middle of India, India as a whole is considered to be a tropical country.

India has three distinct seasons:

- Summer-from March to June
- Rainy (Monsoon)-from June to October
- Winter-from November to March

Winter months are bright and pleasant, with snowfall in the northern hills. Summer time is hot in most parts of India, and it is then that the numerous hill resorts provide cool retreat. During the monsoon, rainfall is heavy along the West Coast between June and September, and along the East Coast between mid-October and December.

Indian Standard Time is GMT+5:30

5

World Geography: Applications

You cannot travel on the path until you become the path itself.

—*Buddha*

Introduction

One cannot understand historical developments without understanding geography. The geographic features of the environment, both physical and human, strongly influence the events of history. An understanding of the contemporary world requires an understanding of geography, that is, of the physical and human systems that drive world events. Geographic concepts also help us think clearly about alternative futures and make us wise decision-makers. Thus, studying tourism geography throws light on the development of tourism, until now and into the future, resulting from the interactions among man, the natural environment, and the social system. At an operational level, this boils down to the applications like using geography knowledge and skills to analyze problems and make decisions within a spatial context; for example, geography can be used to examine tourism in a developed or a developing country to identify conflicts over resource use, the relative advantages and disadvantages of tourism to local resident and the costs and benefits of tourism from several points of view (e.g., those of the owner of a diving shop, a hotel maid, a tourist, and a local fisherman).

In their study, geographers use four interrelated approaches:

- Systematic: Groups geographical knowledge into categories that can be explored globally.
- Regional: Examines systematic relationships between categories for a specific region or location on the planet.
- Descriptive: Simply specifies the locations of features and populations.
- Analytical: Asks why we find features and populations in a specific geographic area.

Maps and Cartography

A map is a picture or representation of the Earth's surface, showing how things are related to each other by distance, direction, and size. Maps are a way of showing many things about a portion of the earth's surface, usually, on a flat piece of paper that can be carried and transported easily. A map is not a photograph of the Earth's surface. It can show many things that a picture cannot show, and as a result, a map looks different in many ways from a photograph of the Earth's surface. Maps have been used for centuries.

A person who creates map as a profession is called a cartographer. Cartography studies the representation of the Earth's surface with abstract symbols (map making). Although other sub-disciplines of geography rely on maps for presenting their analyses, the actual making of maps is abstract enough to be regarded separately. Cartography has grown from a collection of drafting techniques into an actual science. Cartographers must learn cognitive psychology and ergonomics to understand which symbols convey information about the Earth most effectively, and behavioral psychology to induce the readers of their maps to act on the information. They must learn geodesy and fairly advanced mathematics to understand how the shape of the Earth affects the distortion of map symbols projected onto a flat surface for viewing. It can be said, without much controversy, that cartography is the seed from which the larger field of geography grew.

There has always been a direct relationship between tourism and cartography. Maps of travel routes and general information about the areas to visit are used in selecting the destination and in planning travel and stay. In the era of internet and wireless communications, maps have become essential interactive travel guides.

Some of the maps important for tourism geographers are:

Topographic maps show a 3 dimensional world in 2 dimensions by using contour lines. Many people have trouble reading these maps, because they have mountains and valleys are represented with concentric circles and lines. Many hikers use topographic maps, especially in areas where there are no roads with signs.

Road maps show major—some minor highways—and roads, airports, railroad tracks, cities and other points of interest in an area. People use road maps to plan trips and for driving directions.

Climate maps give general information about the climate and precipitation (rain and snow) of a region. Cartographers, or mapmakers, use colors to show different climate or precipitation zones.

Environmental maps look at human's activity in urban and metropolitan areas and the environment in which we all live. *Physical maps* form a subset of this and illustrate the physical features of an area, such as the mountains, rivers and lakes. The water is usually shown in blue. Colors are used to show relief—differences in land elevations.

Political maps do not show physical features. Instead, they indicate state and national boundaries and capital and major cities.

Economic or resource maps feature the type of natural resources or economic activity that dominates an area. Cartographers use symbols to show the locations of natural resources or economic activities.

As spatial interrelationships are key to the science of geography, maps are a key tool. Classical cartography has been joined by more modern approaches to geographical analysis, mainly, computer-based Geographic Information Systems (GIS). In fact, the earliest version of a GIS was known as computer cartography and involved simple line-work to represent land features. From that evolved the concept of overlaying different mapped features on top of each other to determine patterns and causes of spatial phenomenon.

Geographic Information Systems

Geographic information systems (GIS) are a set of computer programs for capturing, storing, checking, integrating, analyzing, and displaying data about the earth. GIS applications involve the storage of information about the Earth for automatic retrieval by a computer, in an accurate manner appropriate to the information's purpose. Thus, in addition to all of the other sub-disciplines of geography, GIS specialists must understand computer science and database systems. GIS has revolutionized the field of cartography; nearly all mapmaking is now done with the assistance of some form of GIS software.

Geostatistics deal with quantitative analysis of the data collected mostly using GIS, specifically the application of statistical methodology to the exploration of geographic phenomena. Geostatistics can be used for tourism planning, especially in those destination areas where there exists competition for land and other resources among industries. Geographic qualitative methods, or ethnographical; research techniques, is the qualitative counterpart of Geostatistics. These techniques are used by human geographers. In cultural geography there is a tradition of employing qualitative research techniques that are also used in anthropology and sociology. Participant observation and in-depth interviews provide human geographers with qualitative data.

The power of a GIS comes from the ability to relate different information in a spatial context and to reach a conclusion about this relationship. Most of the information we have about our world contains a location reference, placing that information at some point on the globe.

So far, a GIS application in tourism has been limited to making digital base maps of printed maps and making digital files for mobile as well as internet mapping. Yet, the potential of GIS in making interactive maps for independent travelers and as informational inputs to

Global Positioning System is increasingly being recognized. In this way, GIS can assist travelers to locate their present spot in a city, the different routs available to another spot, the traffic congestion and any other anomalies in each of these routes, the important landmarks and essential utilities available on a highway, and so on.

Some of the widely used GIS softwares are: GRASS, MapServer, ArcInfo, MapInfo, Autodesk, Caliper, CARIS, Oracle Spatial, Smallworld, etc. Some of these are open source softwares while the others are proprietary or commercial.

Wilderness Tourism

Wilderness may be defined as a land that has not been significantly modified by direct or indirect human activity. The area is managed to maintain its primeval character and influence. It is an area which, together with its plant and animal communities, is in a state that has not been substantially modified or is capable of being restored to such a state; is of a sufficient size to make its maintenance in such a state feasible; and is capable of providing opportunities for recreation. Wilderness provides aesthetic, cultural or scientific significance. Wilderness travel involves personal recreation through primitive travel in natural environments that are devoid of human disturbance. Wilderness-based tourism experiences are increasingly popular given both the growing demand for special interest travel products and tourists' desire to engage with nature.

In the following figure, areas offering wilderness experiences at four different levels are presented on an environmental continuum:

Urban	Urban fringe	Rural	Back country			Remote	Wilderness
			Drive access	4x4 access	Walking		
Settled land		Undeveloped land of increasing primitiveness					
No wilderness quality		Increasing degrees of wilderness quality					
		Low			Medium		High
Level 1:		Wilderness areas of pristine ecology (if they still exist) —>					
Level 2:							Phenomenal wilderness
Level 3:							Legal wilderness
Level 4:		Perceptual wilderness (also known as psychological and sociological)					

At the first level, wilderness may be defined as areas of pristine ecology that are completely free of any human disturbance, and are rare to find. Coming to Level 2, the term phenomenal as relating to phenomena, describes the fact that wilderness may be defined as a stated and mappable physical reality. In these terms, wilderness may be defined as areas where the imprint of humanity is largely unnoticeable. This could probably include wilderness areas that are large enough to traverse on foot in no less than two days and have no developments such as huts, bridges, tracks and signs, and with no provision made for mechanized access. Legal wilderness, the Level 3, describes the fact that wilderness is defined in enactments of legislation. Legal wilderness areas appear to be affected primarily by the forces of nature, have outstanding opportunities for solitude, and have ecological or geological value or features of scientific, education, scenic or historical value. Research in the field of wilderness has led to growing recognition of the need to appreciate the wilderness perceptions of visitors in order to manage relevant recreation resources. This is shown in the figure as Level 4. The concept of wilderness operates both objectively and subjectively. The important ways in which subjective evaluations and interpretations control perceptions of objective environments have been noticed and has become another basic for wilderness classification.

Wilderness travel provides psychological and physical benefits by experiencing wild areas with a minimum of development influences. Nature must be free of the soiling influences of modern peoples. The search is for personal redemption through challenge and sacrifice, and nature is the backdrop to an intensely personal experience. The primary environmental attitudes of wilderness travelers concern knowing and experiencing wild nature. This nature, ideally, should not contain humans, except for a select few. Nature must be unfettered. People must only experience this wild environment in a non-technological form. Human power is the primary form of travel.

Wilderness users are found to be predominantly young males with high levels of formal education. People in the older age groups, such as retirees, have lower levels of participation, probably because of the high levels of physical activity required. Moderately high income groups dominate this segment. Because there is strong and continuous dedication to the activity, the average wilderness user has high levels of previous experience.

Wilderness users have the most coherent and developed set of philosophical treatises of any outdoor group. The roots of their concern go deep into the early Judea Christian idea of seeking re-creation in the wilderness so that the challenges of life can be better met. In India, the philosophy of wilderness visits connotes with the attempts of man to realize oneself with nature. Another perspective, more secular indeed, looks at wilderness as a place where people visit but do not remain, where they enter for only short periods, and where they seek personal re-creation through the challenge posed by free nature. In any case, Wilderness advocacy has become a favorite of the intelligentsia, and social diffusion has spread the idea from the literati.

Tourism is important for the conservation of wilderness. In wilderness areas which are already protected, commercial tourism is growing in scale, and in some cases has become a significant source of anthropogenic impact, and a major logistic and financial issue for land managers. For wilderness outside protected areas, tourism offers an economically valuable land use whose environmental impacts, though by no means negligible, are far less than those of alternative land uses such as logging, farming and fisheries. Tourism is hence a very important tool for wilderness conservation, albeit one whose use is fraught with danger. Inside protected areas, tourism has more environmental impacts than conservation alone, and tourism and recreation need to be managed to maintain the primary conservation value of the area concerned.

That is, wilderness tourism is not to be promoted regardless of the concerns on sustainability. The permission to visit a wilderness area is not a condition free license granted to destroy the very same flora, fauna, and pristine natural forms that give the authentic wilderness experience. While the very act of managing wilderness will dilute the touristic experience (since management of wilderness is likely to generate awareness, recommendation and patterns of use where as authentic wilderness experience requires autonomy, spontaneity, freedom of action and, for some perhaps, mental and physical challenge with a certain degree of risk), it is necessary due to the self-centric economizers that typical tourists are. Theory of the 'Tragedy of the Commons' suggests that freedom of the commons results, in situations of increasing demand, only in ruin for all. The development of access and an upsurge in demand for wilderness experiences has, in many cases, made strict management and use restriction inevitable.

Wilderness tourism is a large market in the United States, which has the most people with this activity profile and also has the most wilderness destinations. Canada is developing many wilderness areas because of the actions of internal wilderness advocate groups, and they are preparing for an increasing number of United States wilderness travelers. Though there exists ample opportunities for countries like India to promote wilderness tourism, nothing concrete and concerted has yet taken place from the side of any major stakeholders.

National Parks

A national park is a reserve of land, usually declared and owned by a national government, protected from most human development and pollution. Their aims are to conserve and enhance the natural beauty, wildlife and cultural heritage they contain, and to promote opportunities and enjoyment by the public of the areas they cover. Born as a dream of profit from limitless recreational tourism, the creation of national parks was an attempt to resolve the conflict over how to wrest the greatest good and profit from the land: consumption through private exploitation or through public tourism.

National parks are a protected area of International Union for the Conservation of Nature (IUCN) category II. According to IUCN, "natural parks are there to protect outstanding natural and scenic areas of national or international significance for scientific, educational, and recreational use. These are relatively large natural areas not materially altered by human activity where extractive resource uses are not allowed". The area must also be entirely controlled by a top ranking government organization which can exercise its power to prohibit any type of development or occupancy throughout the designated park area or to undertake any type of restriction or measures required to effectively maintain the area in terms of preserving the ecosystem, geology, and the scenery.

National parks are found in most countries. There is a great variety of national parks because each nation creates its own approach to suit its own needs. But all national parks have the following common features:

- They identify areas of land or sea—usually extensive areas—which are of the very highest value to the nation for their scenery and wildlife, and often for their cultural heritage value;
- They provide positive management and additional resources to safeguard the special qualities of these areas for the long term; and
- They provide opportunities for the public to enjoy these areas, because they are usually highly attractive places to visit.

National parks have been established by nations to deliver better management of some of the nations' most special areas of outstanding natural and cultural heritage. In operational terms, they have, inter alia, the following aims:

- to conserve and enhance the natural and cultural heritage
- to promote the sustainable use of the natural resources of the area
- to promote understanding and enjoyment (including enjoyment in the form of recreation) of the special qualities of the area by the public
- to promote sustainable social and economic development of the communities of the area

Normally, for each national park, there will be National Park Authority. The main purpose of the National Park Authority is to prepare and facilitate the implementation of the National Park Plan. To do this, each Park Authority will need to work in close partnership with the many stakeholders in the Park, including its communities, its landowners and managers, and other organizations and individuals with an interest in the conservation, enjoyment, understanding and sustainable use of its natural and cultural heritage. In addition, the Park Authority will have a number of functions and powers to help it directly facilitate the achievement of Park aims. These include functions and powers to:

I. Enter into management agreements, make bylaws and establish management rules

II. Make charges for goods and services

III. Provide advice and assistance and undertake or fund research

IV. Provide grant

VI. Purchase land

VII. Create nature reserves

VIII. Provide information and education

IX. Provide countryside facilities such as toilets, car parks, campsites and picnic areas

X. Provide sport, recreation and leisure facilities

XI. Make improvements to inland waterways

XII. Protect and maintain of rights of way; and

XIII. Request traffic management schemes

However, these functions may vary from country to country and from one type of the national park to the other.

In India, the national parks spread across the country offer a fascinating diversity of terrain, flora and fauna. India has preserved vast tracts of forests and habitats in its 80 National Parks and 441 Wildlife Sanctuaries. Each National park is famous for its Wildlife Population. Depending on the area and terrain national parks provide ample opportunities to the visitors to have a close encounters with the wilds.

These aims will be pursued collectively, so that the achievement of one aim for the area will not undermine the achievement of another but should contribute to it. In this way, social and economic development will be addressed alongside the proper protection of the natural heritage. However, in cases where there appears to be irreconcilable conflict between these aims, priority will be given the protection of the area's natural and cultural heritage.

A brief description of some of the national parks is given below:

Bandipur National Park India: Bandipur National Park is a beautiful forest reserve located in the southern Indian state of Karnataka. This national park occupies a special place in India's efforts towards natural conservation. It was created in the 1930s from the local Maharaja Voodiyar's hunting lands, and named Venugopal National Park.

Bharatpur National Park India: The Bharatpur National Park or as many people prefer to call it Keoladeo Ghana National park lies between two of India's most historic cities, Agra and Jaipur. This national park of India is situated in the northwestern state of Rajasthan, about 190 km from the national capital of Delhi.

Corbett National Park India: The Corbett National Park is a primal jungle as Rudyard Kipling put it. Despite extensive tourism, this national park of India has managed to retain its primeval ambience, where man must walk timorously, in awe and with a strong sense of his own insignificance.

Kanha National Park India: Situated in the Indian state of Madhya Pradesh, the picturesque Kanha National Park was the inspiration behind Rudyard Kipling's unforgettable classic Jungle Book. The romance of the Kanha National Park has not reduced over time-it is still as beautiful.

Kaziranga National Park India: Kaziranga National Park, situated in the northeastern state of Assam, is one of the most picturesque wildlife parks in India. The natural habitat of the one-horned rhino, Kaziranga lies on the southern banks of the Brahmaputra River, northeast of Assam's capital Guwahati.

Manas National Park India: Manas National Park situated amidst the gentle slopes at the foothills of the Himalayas in India's northeastern state of Assam, is the only tiger reserve of its kind in the entire northeast.

Nagarhole National Park India: Nagarhole National park derives its name from the combination of two Kannada words 'Nagar,' meaning snake, and 'hole,' meaning streams. True to its name, quite a few serpentine streams fork through the rich tropical forests of the national park.

Periyar National Park India: Situated within the confines of the Western Ghats in the southern Indian state of Kerala, Periyar National Park and Tiger Reserve is one of the most captivating wildlife parks in the world.

Sariska National Park India: Sariska National Park (near Alwar) is situated in the state of Rajasthan in the backdrop of the Aravali Hills. This national park, which is quite near to Rajasthan's capital Jaipur, was declared a sanctuary in 1955.

Silent Valley National Park India: Located in the Kundali Hills of the Western Ghats, the Silent Valley National Park holds a valuable reserve of rare plants and herbs. The park is rich in its wildlife, and elephants lion-tailed macaques and tigers are the most common denizens of this national park.

Simlipal National Park India: Simlipal national park originated primarily as a hunting ground for the royalty It was formally designated a tiger reserve in 1956 under Project Tiger in May 1972. It was elevated to a national park status in 1979.

Sunderbans National Park India: Situated south of Calcutta, Sunderbans National Park is one of the most unique ecosystems in this part of the world and is dominated by mangrove forests. A UNESCO world heritage site, Sunderbans National Park is home to the largest number of wild tigers in the world.

The following is a list of all national parks in India

Name	*State*
Anshi National Park	Karnataka
Balphakram National Park	Meghalaya
Bandhavgarh National Park	Madhya Pradesh
Bandipur National Park	Karnataka
Bannerghatta National Park	Karnataka
Vansda National Park	Gujarat
Betla National Park	Jharkhand
Bhitarkanika National Park	Orissa
Blackbuck National Park	Gujarat
Buxa Tiger Reserve	West Bengal
Campbell Bay National Park	Andaman and Nicobar
Corbett National Park	Uttaranchal
Dachigam National Park	Jammu and Kashmir

Desert National Park	Rajasthan
Dibru-Saikhowa Park	Assam
Dudhwa National Park	Uttar Pradesh
Eravikulam National Park	Kerala
Fossil National Park	Madhya Pradesh
Galathea National Park	Andaman and Nicobar
Gangotri National Park	Uttaranchal
Gir National Park	Gujarat
Gorumara National Park	West Bengal
Govind Pashu Vihar	Uttaranchal
Great Himalayan Park	Himachal Pradesh
Gugamal National Park	Maharashtra
Guindy National Park	Tamil Nadu
Gulf of Kachchh Park	Gujarat
Gulf of Mannar Park	Tamil Nadu
Hemis National Park	Jammu and Kashmir
Indira Gandhi National Park	Tamil Nadu
Indravati National Park	Chhattisgarh
Intanki National Park	Nagaland
Kalesar National Park	Haryana
Kanha National Park	Madhya Pradesh
Kanger Ghati National Park	Chhattisgarh
Kasu Reddy National Park	Andhra Pradesh
Kaziranga National Park	Assam
Keibul Lamjao Park	Manipur
Keoladeo National Park	Rajasthan
Khangchendzonga Park	Sikkim
Kishtwar National Park	Jammu and Kashmir
Kudremukh National Park	Karnataka
Madhav National Park	Madhya Pradesh
Mahatma Gandhi Park	Andaman and Nicobar
Mahavir Vanasthali Park	Andhra Pradesh
Manas National Park	Assam
Mathikettan Shola Park	Kerala
Middle Button Island Park	Andaman and Nicobar
Mollem National Park	Goa
Mouling National Park	Arunachal Pradesh

Mount Abu Sanctuary	Rajasthan
Mount Harriet National Park	Andaman and Nicobar
Mrugavani National Park	Andhra Pradesh
Mudumalai National Park	Tamil Nadu
Mukurthi National Park	Tamil Nadu
Murlen National Park	Mizoram
Nagarhole National Park	Karnataka
Namdapha National Park	Arunachal Pradesh
Nameri National Park	Assam
Nanda Devi Biosphere	Uttaranchal
Navegaon National Park	Maharashtra
Neora Valley National Park	West Bengal
Nokrek National Park	Meghalaya
North Button Island Park	Andaman and Nicobar
Orang National Park	Assam
Panna National Park	Madhya Pradesh
Pench National Park	Madhya Pradesh
Pench National Park	Maharashtra
Periyar National Park	Kerala
Phawngpui Mountain Park	Mizoram
Pin Valley National Park	Himachal Pradesh
Rajaji National Park	Uttaranchal
Rajiv Gandhi National Park	Rajasthan
Rani Jhansi Marine Park	Andaman and Nicobar
Ranthambore National Park	Rajasthan
Saddle Peak National Park	Andaman and Nicobar
Salim Ali National Park	Jammu and Kashmir
Sanjay National Park[2]	Chhattisgarh
Sanjay National Park[2]	Madhya Pradesh
Sanjay Gandhi National Park	Maharashtra
Sariska National Park	Rajasthan
Satpura National Park	Madhya Pradesh
Silent Valley National Park	Kerala
Sirohi National Park	Manipur
Simlipal National Park	Orissa

Singalila National Park	West Bengal
South Button Island Park	Andaman and Nicobar
Sri Venkateswara Park	Andhra Pradesh
Sultanpur National Park	Haryana
Sundarbans National Park	West Bengal
Tadoba National Park	Maharashtra
Valley of Flowers Park	Uttaranchal
Valmiki National Park	Bihar
Van Vihar National Park	Madhya Pradesh

Tourism Impacts

Tourism, with its development, generates benefits and curses which are otherwise known as positive and negative impacts, respectively. The impacts are mainly received by the society and culture, economy, and the natural environment. Tourism impact studies analyze the impacts of tourism upon the different stakeholders that are party to tourism.

Not all impacts are applicable to every community because conditions or resources differ. Tourism policies must also balance the opportunities and concerns of all community sectors by working against conditions where positive impacts benefit one part of the community and negative impacts hurt another. Ideally, a final decision with regard to tourism development is a community should be taken only if the social benefits are maximized and the social cost controlled to the least.

One can see tourism as an interaction among the three major groupings of the community, the tourism industry, and the tourists themselves. In the language of cost-benefit analysis (CBA), tourism costs and benefits may be expressed in terms of the following inequalities:

i. CB>IB>IC>CC (The inequality of interaction between the community and the industry)

ii. CB>TB>TC>CC (The inequality of interaction between the community and the tourists)

iii. IB>TB>TC>IC (The inequality of interaction between the industry and the tourists)

(CB=Community Benefits; CC=Community Costs; IB=Industrial Benefits; IC=Industrial Costs; TB=Tourist Benefits; and TC=Tourist Costs)

Note that the maximum benefit with the least cost goes to the community. This is the essential condition for sustainable tourism and the other conditions are not as consequential as this. The third condition may even be contested; however, we feel this is desirable since only if the industry benefit is significant than the industry cost shall it survive and not move on to unsustainable practices; tourists shall visit a destination as long as tourist benefit is more than tourist cost.

Conflicts among the different stakeholder groups take place due to each one's divergent interests. Hence, the best way to avoid conflict of interests is to plan for increasing the overlapping interests and decreasing the divergent interests.

Now, let us examine the different types of impacts in more depth (Adapted from Kreag, G., 2001):

The Socio-Cultural Impact: The social and cultural ramifications of tourism warrant careful consideration, as impacts can either become assets or detriments to communities. Influxes of tourists bring diverse values to the community and influence behaviors and family life. Individuals and the collective community might try to please tourists or adopt tourist behaviors. Interactions between residents and tourists can impact creative expression by providing new opportunities (positive) or by stifling individuality with new restrictions (negative).

Increased tourism can push a community to adopt a different moral conduct such as improved understanding between sexes (positive) or increased illicit drug use (negative). Safety and health facilities and staffing tend to increase at the same time safety problems such as crime and accidents increase. Traditional ceremonies may be renewed and revived by tourist interest or lost in alternative activities. Community organizations can be invigorated by facing the opportunities of tourism or overwhelmed by its associated problems. Calamities such as natural disasters, energy shortages, terrorism, political upheaval, disease outbreak, a chemical spill, or even widespread negative publicity could shut down tourism abruptly but sometimes can attract curious visitors. Tourism can improve the quality of life in an area by increasing the number of attractions, recreational opportunities, and services. Tourism offers the residents opportunities to meet interesting people, make friendships, learn about the world, and expose themselves to new perspectives. Experiencing different cultural practices enriches experiences, broadens horizons, and increases insight and appreciation for different approaches to living. Often, dwindling interest in host cultures is revived by reawakening cultural heritage as part of tourism development, which increases demand for historical and cultural exhibits. This interest by tourists in local culture and history provides opportunities to support preservation of historical artifacts and architecture. By learning more about others, their differences become less threatening and more interesting. At the same time, tourism often promotes higher levels of psychological satisfaction from opportunities created by tourism development and through interactions with travelers. Tourism can come to a community with a dark social and cultural side, too. Illegal activities tend to increase in the relaxed atmosphere of tourist areas. Increased underage drinking can become a problem especially in beach communities, areas with festivals involving alcohol, and ski villages. It is easier to be anonymous where strangers are taken for granted; bustling tourist traffic can increase the presence of smugglers and buyers of smuggled products. Lifestyle changes such as alterations in local travel patterns to avoid tourist congestion and the avoidance of downtown shopping can damage a community socially and culturally. Hotels, restaurants, and shops can push tourism development into residential areas, forcing changes in the physical structure of a community. Development of tourist facilities in prime locations may cause locals to be or feel excluded from those resources. As local ethnic culture alters to fit the needs of tourism, language and cultural practices may change. The „demonstration effect" of tourists (residents adopting tourist behaviors) and the addition of tourist facilities may alter customs, such as dating habits, especially those of a more structured or traditional culture. The potential of meeting and marrying non-local mates may create family stress.

The Economic Impact

Tourism increases employment opportunities. Additional jobs, ranging from low-wage entry-level to high-paying professional positions in management and technical fields, generate income and raise standards of living. Particularly in rural areas, the diversification created by tourism helps communities that are possibly dependent on only one industry. As tourism grows, additional opportunities are created for investment, development, and infrastructure spending. Tourism often induces improvements in public utilities such as water, sewer, sidewalks, lighting, parking, public restrooms, litter control, and landscaping. Such improvements benefit tourists and residents alike. Likewise, tourism encourages improvements in transport infrastructure resulting in upgraded roads, airports, public transportation, and non-traditional transportation. Tourism encourages new elements to join the retail mix, increasing opportunities for shopping and adding healthy competitiveness. It often increases a community's tax revenues. Lodging and sales taxes most notably increase but additional tax revenues include air travel and other transportation taxes, business taxes, and fuel taxes. New jobs generate more income tax revenues. When considering the economic impacts of tourism, it is essential to understand that tourism businesses often include a significant number of low-paying jobs, often at minimum wage or less. These jobs are often seasonal, causing under-employment or unemployment during off-seasons. Labor may be imported, rather than hired locally, especially if particular skills or expertise is required, or if local labor is unavailable. Some tourism-related businesses are volatile and high-risk ventures that are unsustainable. Greater demand for goods, services, land, and housing may increase prices that in turn will increase the cost of living. Tourism businesses may claim land that could have higher- value or other uses. Additionally, non-local owners and corporations may export profits out of the community. The community may have to generate funds to maintain roads and transportation systems that have become more heavily used. Similarly, if additional infrastructure is required, additional taxes may also be needed to pay for them.

The Environmental Impact

Areas with high-value natural resources, like oceans, lakes, waterfalls, mountains, unique flora and fauna, and great scenic beauty attract tourists and new residents (in-migrants) who seek emotional and spiritual connections with nature. Because these people value nature, selected natural environments are preserved, protected, and kept from further ecological decline. Lands that could be developed can generate income by accommodating the recreational activities of visitors. Tourist income often makes it possible to preserve and restore historic buildings and monuments. Improvements in the area's appearance through cleanup or repairs and the addition of public art such as murals, water fountains, and monuments benefit visitors and residents alike. Tourism is generally considered a „clean" industry, one that is based on hotels, restaurants, shops and attractions, instead of factories. Tourism can also degrade an environment. Visitors generate waste and pollution (air, water, solid waste, noise, and visual). Natural resource attractions can be jeopardized through improper uses or overuse. Providing tourist services can alter the landscape's appearance. For instance, visual pollution may occur from billboard proliferation. As tourism develops, demand for land increases, especially for prime locations like beachfronts, special views, and mountains. Without forethought, natural landscape and open space can be lost. The destruction or loss of flora and fauna can happen when desirable plants and animals are collected for sale or the land is trampled. Tourists or the businesses that cater to them often remove plants, animals, rocks, fossils, coral, and cultural or historical artifacts from an area. Uncontrolled visitation or overuse by visitors can degrade landscapes, historic sites, and monuments. Where water is scarce, tourists can overwhelm the available supply. Travelers can also inadvertently introduce non-indigenous species, as can increases in the trade of animals and plants. A constant stream of visitors and domestic pets may disrupt wildlife by disturbing their breeding cycles and altering natural behaviors.

Some of the major impacts of tourism are summarized below:

Type of Impact	*Positive Impacts*	*Negative Impacts*
Socio-Cultural	•Improves quality of life •Facilitates meeting visitors (educational experience) •Positive changes in values and customs •Promotes cultural exchange •Improves understanding of different communities •Preserves cultural identity of host population •Increases demand for historical and cultural exhibits •Greater tolerance of social differences •Satisfaction of psychological needs	•Excessive drinking, alcoholism, gambing •Increased underage drinking •Crime, drugs, prostitution •Increased smuggling •Language and cultural effects •Unwanted lifestyle changes •Displacement of residents for tourism development •Negative changes in values and customs •Family disruption •Exclusion of locals from natural resources •New cliques modify social structure
Economic	•Contributes to income and standard of living •Improves local economy •Increases employment opportunities •Improves investment, development, and infrastructure	•Increases price of goods and services •Increases price of land and housing •Increases cost of living •Increases potential for imported labor

spending	•Increases tax revenues •Improves public utilities infrastructure •Improves transport infrastructure •Increases opportunities for shopping •Creates new business opportunities	•Cost for additional infrastructure (Water, power, medical, etc.) •Increases road maintenance and transportation system costs •Seasonal tourism creates high-risk, under or unemployment issues •Competition for land with other (higher value) economic uses •Profits may be exported by non-local owners •Jobs may pay low wages
Environmental	•Protection of selected natural environments or prevention of further ecological decline •Preservation of historic buildings and monuments •Improvement of the area's appearance (visual and aesthetic) •A smokeless industry	•Pollution (air, water, noise, solid waste, and visual) •Loss of natural landscape and agricultural lands to tourism development •Loss of open space •Destruction of flora and fauna (including plants, animals, rocks, coral, or artifacts) •Degradation of landscape, historic sites, and monuments •Water shortages •Introduction of exotic species and mono culture •Disruption of wildlife breeding cycles and behaviors

Destination Carrying Capacity

Destination carrying capacity may be defined as the number of people that a destination area can support given the quality of the natural environment and the level of technology of the population. The World Tourism Organization (WTO) defines the concept of carrying capacity as follows: "The maximum number of people that may visit a tourist destination at the same time, without causing destruction of the physical, economic and socio-cultural environment and an unacceptable decrease in the quality of the visitors' satisfaction".

The concept of carrying capacity is often presented as a particularly useful approach for determining the intensity of tourism development that can be supported by a region, considering its economic, ecological and social characteristics. At least 4 different types of carrying capacities have been identified in the literature:

Physical carrying capacity—the limit of a site beyond which wear and tear will start taking place or environmental problems will arise

Psychological (or perceptual or aesthetic) carrying capacity—the lowest degree of enjoyment tourists are prepared to accept before they start seeking alternative destinations

Social carrying capacity—the level of tolerance of the host population for the presence and behavior of tourists in the destination area, and/or the degree of crowding users (tourists) are prepared to accept by others (other tourists)

Economic carrying capacity—the ability to absorb tourism activities without displacing or disrupting desirable local activities

Until now, only few attempts have been made to operationalize this concept and to transform it into a management tool for the persons in charge of tourism destinations. Many experts feel that it is difficult to quantify carrying capacity since it involves a lot of intangible aspects. Thus, instead of providing a universally applicable formula, it is better to provide a framework within which carrying capacity may be calculated. Such a broad framework can be used as a reference document, but the final output and conclusions will depend on the nature of each study area and its values. A framework provided by Lim, L.C. (1995) is provided below (more details available at FAO Corporate Document Repository):

Carrying Capacity Measurement

1. Define the carrying capacity that needs to be established for the study area:

Options:
- tourism carrying capacity
- recreation carrying capacity
- others

Consider the above from one or more of the following perspectives:

- physical carrying capacity
- ecological carrying capacity
- social carrying capacity
- economic carrying capacity

Consider factors that affect the overall capacity of an area:

Options:
- access capacity
- commercial capacity
- construction capacity
- service capacity
- transport capacity
- others

2. Consider the type of tourism existing or being planned from the following contexts:

- physical
- social
- cultural
- infrastructure
- economic benefits
- tourism image
- indigenous environment
- others

3. List the objectives of the area:

Options:
- conservation of natural resources
- preservation of areas of unique scientific, historical and cultural value
- preservation of heritage
- tourism and recreation
- employment opportunities
- others

Ecological and social consequences of use should be consistent with area management objectives. If an area has more than one objective, then state the objective of highest priority.

4. Establish criteria that affect capacity:

(a) Physical:
- area size
- accessible space
- visual impact
- climate
- aesthetics
- accommodation quality
- availability of facilities
- transportation

	• number of people that can be accommodated • others
(b) Ecological:	• the need for conservation • fragility of the environment • wildlife resources • topography • vegetative cover • behavioral sensitivity of species • diversity • uniqueness of species • concealment • resilience of ecosystem/species • impact of use on the area • others
For coral reefs, the following must also be taken into account:	
	• size and shape of reef: • composition of coral communities: • type of underwater activity: • level of experience of divers/snorkellers: • others:
(c) Economic:	• investment • volume of tourists • cost of the holiday • level of economic benefits provided • level of enjoyment suited to the residents • others
(d) Cultural:	• volume of tourism with no detrimental effects • cultural attractions • quality of crafts and food • involvement of local communities/residents • others
(e) Social:	• visitors' choice • visitors' opinions • visitors' attitude and behavior • expectations and preferences • perceptual and behavioral response • response to rising use levels • visitors' activities • visitor satisfaction

- acceptable level of crowding
- involvement of local communities/residents
- others

(f) Availability of resources and infrastructure:	• cash incentives • public utilities • transport facilities • essential facilities e.g. hospitals • availability of water supply • proper disposal of solid and liquid wastes • others
(g) Administrative and political factors:	• level at which management is implemented • legal restraints • policy incentives • others

5. Establish thresholds or tolerable levels of use that can act as management guidelines:

Options:	• physical • economic • ecological • perceptual • social/cultural • political/administrative • others

6. Assess the carrying capacity of the area:

(a) Physical carrying capacity

(i) Consider in terms of time and space variables, and tourist function rates.

Time:	• peak capacity • daily capacity • weekly capacity • yearly capacity • seasonal and diurnal • others
Space:	• space coefficients • unit measures • density zones

	• equipment ratios • others
Tourist function rates:	• ratios • others
Threshold capacities:	• economic viability • water resources • others
Non-measurable criteria (use comparative analyses):	• ecological impacts • cultural impacts • psychological effects • others

(ii) Apply the formula.

- $$\text{Carrying capacity} = \frac{\text{Area used by tourists}}{\text{Average individual standard}}$$

The total number of allowed daily visits is then obtained:

- Total daily visits = Carrying capacity x Rotation coefficient

The rotation coefficient is thus determined:

- $$\text{Rotation coefficient} = \frac{\text{No. of daily hours area is open for tourists}}{\text{Average time of visit}}$$

(b) Social carrying capacity

(i) Establish conditions requiring judgmental inputs:

- Relationship between use levels/management parameters and experience parameters
- Agreement about the type of recreational experience to be provided
- Agreement about the appropriate levels of experience parameters

(ii) Document visitor particulars and activities, as well as their expectations and preferences. Then a theoretical evaluation based on experience and accumulated knowledge can be used for comparative analyses.

Options:	• frequency of site visits • group size • length of stay • activity patterns • expectations and preferences • others

(c) Ecological carrying capacity

(i) Consider the level of ecological use the area can support.

(ii) Consider if factors such as the following are at risk:

- soil erosion
- pollution of water resources
- landslides
- loss of species
- others

(iii) Assess the capability of the area to cope with increased water demand and waste disposal.

(d) Recreation carrying capacity (requires an assessment of both environmental and social capacities)

(i) Apply the ROS process to establish the acceptable numbers of visitors suited to each zone:

- Visitor surveys
- Density guidelines
- Others

(ii) Describe observable characteristics and carry out

evaluation which involves judgments on acceptability of impacts:

Description:	• management parameters • impact parameters
Evaluation:	• measurable • non-measurable • absolute • empirical terms • others

Carrying Capacity Management And Implementation Guidelines

1. Consider the stage of the tourism life cycle that the area is in, and manage accordingly:

Options:	• exploration stage • growth/development stage • mature/consolidation stage • decline stage

2. Zone the area according to its use and objectives, and develop specific management plans for each zone:

For example:	• primitive • rural • suburban • urban • others

3. If in line with management objectives, consider ways to increase the carrying capacity of the area:

Options:	• establish quotas which set numerical limits on visitors • reduce conflict between competing uses • provide adequate information • increase durability of resources • expand the capacities of utility services • expand the capacities of transport facilities • develop purpose-built tourist resort

complexes
- invest in careful design of infrastructure
- access restriction
- activity restriction
- time separation e.g. seasonal closure
- implement speed limits on boats
- ensure amenity features and facilities are available to residents at reasonable costs
- encourage local resident participation in tourism
- others

In addition, there can be the option to disperse pressure on an area by creating alternatives or opening up new areas. This also provides economic benefits of additional income and employment elsewhere.

Options:
- disperse tourist attractions
- develop new attractions and tourist facilities
- design new viewing tracts, trails, etc.
- extend visit season
- encourage wet or off-season use
- others

4. Implement an education program which will help create awareness and educate the public on conservation matters:

Options:
- exhibits and signs
- surface or underwater trails/routes
- guidebooks and brochures
- public awareness program
- others

5. Incorporate all these into a management plan, ensuring that a government mandate is included:

A competent management program should incorporate both environmental considerations *and* human needs and desires.

6. Implement appropriate action at the various levels:

Options:	
	• local • municipal • district • state • federal

7. Monitor and evaluate conditions:

This would enable management policies to be amended if necessary.

Coastal and Marine Tourism

Coastal tourism and recreation belong to one of the evergreen types of tourism. Tourism and recreation-related development is one of the major factors shaping development patterns in the coastal zones of many countries in the world. Coastal tourism embraces the full range of tourism, leisure, and recreationally oriented activities that take place in the coastal zone and the offshore coastal waters. These include coastal tourism development (hotels, resorts, restaurants, food industry, vacation homes, second homes, etc.), and the infrastructure supporting coastal development (retail businesses, marinas, fishing tackle stores, dive shops, fishing piers, recreational boating harbors, beaches, recreational fishing facilities, and the like). Also included are the recreational activities such as recreational boating, cruises, swimming, recreational fishing, snorkeling, diving, and the public and private programs affecting all the aforesaid. Sometimes the terms coastal tourism and marine tourism are used interchangeably. Yet, some argue that marine tourism involves tourism activities in the water where as coastal tourism involves activities in the shore.

Of all the activities that take place in coastal zones

and the near-shore coastal ocean, none is increasing in both volume and diversity more than coastal tourism and recreation. Both the dynamic nature of this sector and its magnitude demand that it be actively taken into account in government plans, policies, and programs related to the coasts and ocean. Indeed, virtually all coastal and ocean issue areas affect coastal tourism and recreation either directly or indirectly. Clean water, healthy coastal habitats, and a safe, secure, and enjoyable environment are clearly fundamental to successful coastal tourism. Similarly, bountiful living marine resources (fish, shellfish, wetlands, coral reefs, etc.) are of critical importance to most recreational experiences. Security from risks associated with natural coastal hazards such as storms, hurricanes, tsunamis, and the like is a requisite for coastal tourism to be sustainable over the long term.

A nation's coasts and coastal waters are of great value to its people both for their personal enjoyment and for the economic benefits these areas generate for coastal communities, coastal states, and for the nation as a whole¾ benefits that can be sustained indefinitely with proper foresight and enlightened public policies. But, these benefits cannot be taken for granted. Coastal habitats and the resources they support must be protected and, wherever necessary, restored. The quality of coastal waters must be maintained at a sufficiently high level to provide a healthy and aesthetically pleasing environment for water-based recreation. Similarly, swimming beaches must be maintained at an attractive and functional level even in the presence of accelerating sea-level rise and associated erosion, and possible increases in the frequency of coastal storms. The maintenance of safe conditions for recreational boating and underwater recreation (e.g., adequately marked waterways, timely weather information, rescue services, hyperbaric chambers, etc.) is also of great importance.

Sustainable development of coastal tourism is dependent on:

1. Good coastal management practices (particularly regarding proper setting of tourism infrastructure and the provision of public access);
2. Clean water and air, and healthy coastal ecosystems;
3. Maintaining a safe and secure recreational environment though the management of coastal hazards (such as erosion, storms, floods), and the provision of adequate levels of safety for boaters, swimmers, and other water users;
4. Beach restoration efforts that maintain the recreational and amenity values of beaches; and,
5. Sound policies for wildlife and habitat protection.

However, promoting coastal and marine tourism has a significant impact upon the coastal and marine environment.

Marine mammals such as whales and dolphins (and more recently seals) are frequently the focus of tourism operations. These engaging and mysterious animals have provided opportunity for the development of marine leisure activities such as whale watching tours. When tourists are involved in wildlife viewing or interaction there is typically an impact on the animals even if at times tourists are unaware of this. The presence of tourist activity can cause a range of direct and indirect impacts on wildlife which include: disturbance leading to modification of activity patterns, habituation, aberrant social behavior, dietary distortions, reduced fitness and reproductive output, increased predation, altered community structures, abandonment of home ranges, and habitat modification and pollution. Tourist disruption to wildlife often results in behavioral changes and probably because it is most easily measured, this issue has been the centre of many investigative studies. Wildlife responses to tourists can range from minor aberrations in normal behavior patterns to clear indicators of agitation or stress such as retreat from tourist vessels. Disturbance from tourists at times involves physiological costs to the impacted animals. Annoyance to marine and coastal birds from tourism has similarly been shown to occur.

Pollution is a by-product of tourism and can cause harmful chemicals or debris to be introduced into plant and animal habitats. Human and machine impacts upon formations like coral reefs and estuaries are also to be noted.

6

Tourism: A Community Based Approach

Community Based Development and Community Based Tourism

Community-based development is a strategy used by tourism planners to mobilize communities into action to participate in broadening the scope of offerings in the industry. The goal is socio-economic empowerment and a value-added experience for local and foreign visitors. This process opens new niches for destinations, most notably for the nature, culture, and adventure travelers. What this achieves is a policy objective of creating a culture of inclusion in the industry, whereby communities participate and share in the wealth of the industry, dispelling a long held perception of tourism as an exploiter of wealth where only the rich can benefit.

Community-based development empowers people to be more aware of the value of their community assets - their culture, heritage, cuisine and lifestyle. It mobilizes them to convert these into income generating projects while offering a more diverse and worthwhile experience to visitors. Every citizen is a potential business partner to be trained in small business management, environmental awareness, product development and marketing. This type of 'people-centered' tourism promotes a sense of 'ownership' which augurs well for the industry's sustainability.

Continuing with the above line of thinking, community based tourism (CBT) is may be defined as tourism that takes environmental, social and cultural sustainability into account. It is managed and owned by the community, for the community, with the purpose of enabling visitors to increase their awareness and learn about community and local ways of life. Existing terms like heritage tourism, eco-tourism, agri-tourism, cultural tourism, etc can all be forms of the community tourism product, within the constraint that these are to be promoted with the spirit of community centeredness and sustenance.

The key benefits of CBT are seen to be: job creation; poverty reduction; less impact on an area's culture and environment than that exerted by mass tourism; community capacity building and pride; and revenue for maintaining or upgrading the community's cultural assets. The relationship between resources and actions in CBT is illustrated below:

The key rationale underlying the approach and objectives of CBT for conservation and development is that CBT through increased intensities of participation can provide widespread economic and other benefits and decision-making power to communities. These economic benefits act as incentives for participants and the means to conserve the natural and cultural resources on which income generation depends. Note from the diagram that

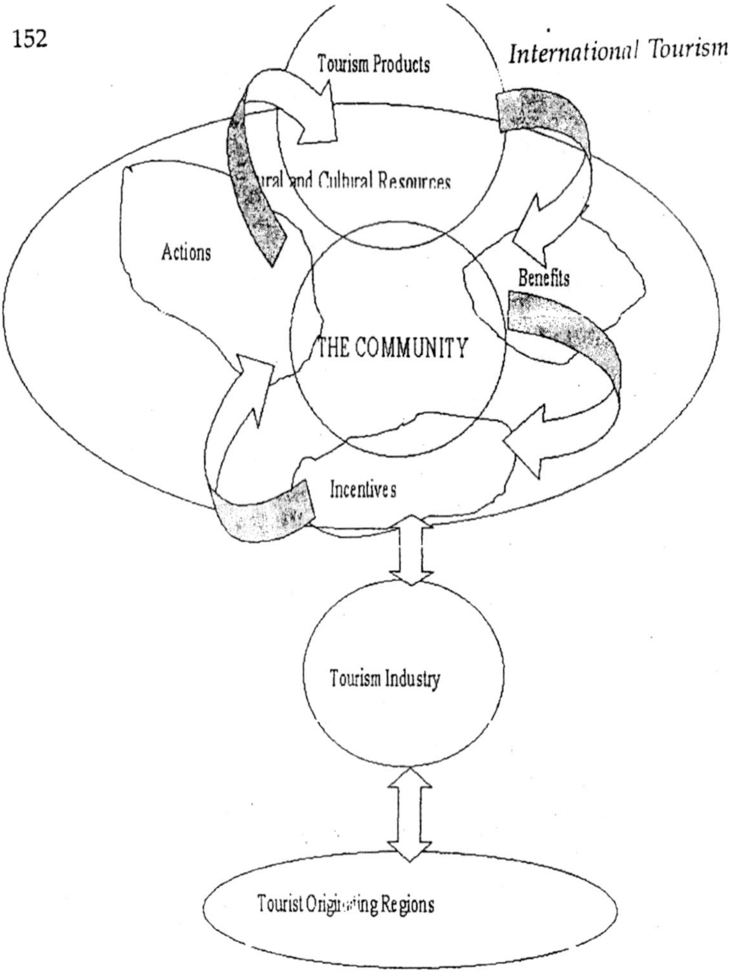

the community is at the centre and is occupying the commanding position with regard to the management of its natural and cultural resources which can be reformulated as tourism products. The relationship of the industry to the tourism products developed out of the natural and cultural resources of the community is not a direct, one-to-one relationship; on the contrary, it is through the intermediation of the community. This is aimed to ensure that the aspirations of the community are never bypassed by the extraneous industry interests. One can see CBT as an interaction among the three major groupings of the community, the tourism industry, and the tourists themselves.

Defining Characteristics of a Community Based Tourism Project

Community-based Tourism can and should encompass a range of activities that collectively contribute to improved conservation and development. Some of the most noteworthy characteristics of community based tourism projects are listed below (adapted from TPDCO, 2005):

- A community-based tourism project is a profitable and sustainable activity that enhances the environment while adding value to the experience of both locals and visitors.
- It directly involves the community – providing both social and economic benefits.
- Its ultimate goal is to satisfy consumer expectations without harming the community interests.
- It is market driven and has to meet high standards in order to be sustainable.
- Private entrepreneurs, community groups, and or organizations may own it. It should aim to educate, train develop, encourage, and utilize any skills and human potential within the community, towards the delivery of professional service.
- It should be operated within a business structure that adheres to government regulations, financial obligations, good labor relations and sound management systems.
- All Business Plans must be scrutinized to ensure owners/organizations understand the

opportunities, pitfalls and risks and to show the long-term viability of the Project.

- Environmental awareness and sustainability should be top priority. It is the responsibility of the community to maintain clean healthy surroundings.
- Members of the community are expected to exhibit friendliness, honesty and professionalism amongst themselves as well as in their dealings with the visitor to ensure the integrity of the project.

Every community based tourism developer must ask the following questions from the very first stage of idea generation for the same:

- Will the project enhance environment while adding value to the visitor's experience?
- Will the project be developed, operated and protected by the community?
- Will the project provide social and economic benefits to the stakeholders/shareholders?
- Will the project be operated with sound ethical business practices including adherence to regulations and standards set by government, agencies, stakeholders, shareholders and consumers?
- Will the project offer professional services and value to the visitor and be competitive in the global marketplace?

If not properly devised and implemented, CBT is highly likely to fail. The International Centre for Responsible Tourism (ICRT) at the University of Greenwich, UK, is evaluating CBT projects around the world and reviewing literature on CBT. Preliminary findings from this research suggest several reasons why CBT projects fail:

- Few projects understand the need for commercial activities: local people must sell crafts, food, accommodation and wildlife or cultural experiences to tourists. This is the only way to ensure a sustainable supply of local income or conservation funds.
- CBT projects must engage with the private sector, including travel agents, tour operators and hoteliers. The earlier this engagement takes place and the closer the partnership, the more likely it is to succeed.
- Location is critical: for poor people to benefit, tourists must stay in or near to these communities. Very few communities have tourism assets which are sufficiently strong to attract tourists - they rely on selling complementary goods and services. Tourists need to be close by for this to happen.
- CBT projects do not always provide appropriate tourism facilities for generating income. For example, too many CBT initiatives rely on building lodges, which are capital intensive and need considerable maintenance, or walking trails from which it can be difficult to secure revenue.
- Protected areas increasingly rely on money from tourists to pay for conservation initiatives. Local communities often have to compete with conservation projects for revenues.

The ICRT summarizes the recipe for successful CBT as that providing:

- Collective benefits: for example providing funds

for community assets such as grinding mills or school books.

- Individual benefits: paid employment (full - or part-time) and opportunities for micro-enterprise earnings (for example craft sales).

The Blueprint for Developing Community Based Tourism in a Destination

In order that CBT be developed in a systematic manner, a methodological framework needs to be adopted. An outline of a suggested framework is provided below (Source: Tuffin, 2005):

1. Choose a destination
2. Complete a feasibility study with the community
3. Create an action plan
4. Set up an administrative system
5. Prepare for operation
6. Monitor and evaluate

Step 1: Choose a destination

Choosing an appropriate destination requires collecting information that leads to an understanding of the community. A detailed study of the village context includes collecting information about the community from organizations working there, government agencies, other communities in the area, and the community members themselves.

Step 2: Complete a feasibility study

The community needs to be fully involved in the process of deciding if they want to be involved in a tourism project. The process for building consensus in the community requires that the information and data be studied with the public and private partners and then an action plan be formulated. It is important to be open and honest about the limitations of the community when deciding whether to continue or not. The decision to develop CBT must be agreed upon by all parties. During this process the community will be stimulated to think about the reasons and motivations for developing CBT. They should be able to discuss the issues and visit communities which are already involved in CBT. The community members need to answer questions like:

Do you want CBT to raise income?

Do you want CBT to preserve culture?

Do you want CBT to conserve natural resources?

Do you want CBT to bring more knowledge and skills into the community?

Step 3: Create an action plan

If all parties reach a consensus, the planning process can begin. In this stage the community creates an action plan and enters into agreement with external agencies like tour operators. Some of the key issues that need to be considered include: Programs for the tourists; Services that will need to be provided; Development of facilities and infrastructure; Training that will need to be provided; Carrying capacity; and, Tour program and price.

The public partner (association of the community members) will need to formulate a monitoring and evaluation plan that includes the associated indicators and the private partner can begin to draft a marketing plan and strategy.

Step 4: Set up an administrative system

Without transparent organization, confusion, suspicion, and conflict can arise in the community. It is crucial that the community sets up a clear administrative system to effectively manage CBT.

The administrative organization will focus on the following: Participation level of community members; Division of roles in operation; Division of benefits; Transparency of management; Measures to control economic and social impacts; Measures to control natural and cultural impacts; and, Cooperation and communication with public and private partners.

Step 5: Preparation of operation

Before full operation of the tour program can start the community and its partners need to acquire skills and experience in operating CBT. The infrastructure must all be designed and built and the equipment acquired and put in place. At this stage emphasis will be placed on:

Training: including guiding skills, language learning, food preparation, housekeeping and simple accounting systems

Preparation of information: involving the educational content of the tour program; the things about themselves that the community members will share with tourists

Infrastructure design and construction: community lodges, trails, water systems, power systems, toilets, etc.

The community members will need to gain experience in guiding and operating the tour program and distributing benefits. It will be necessary to bring pilot groups of tourists into the community so that the community members can see what works and what does not and so that they can practice their skills and test the administrative systems.

Step 6: Monitoring and evaluation

Monitoring and evaluation starts once the program is in full operation. It helps to identify problems, impacts and benefits, as well as to ensure the sustainability of the operation. It examines the extent to which the project is meeting its objectives. It should also result in plans and efforts to compensate for weaknesses, correct problems, adjust systems and improve the program. Monitoring and evaluation is a participatory process. All stakeholders should play a role in gathering the monitoring data, assisting in the analysis, and in actions taken as a result of the final assessment and evaluation.

The aspects monitored include: Environmental impacts; Economic impacts; Cultural impacts; Social impacts; Efficacy of CBT as a development tool; etc.

Information can be gathered from the tourists, the community members and from physical inspections of infrastructure and the environment. Tools used for monitoring can include questionnaires, interviews, focus groups, guest books, photographs, checklists, trend lines, seasonal calendars, and so on.

Often in CBT the locations are remote and subject to national policies regulating access by foreigners as well as domestic visitors. Thus while initial assessments show considerable potential as tourism destinations, there may be regulations that restrict access by numbers and by seasons. International policies and actions have complex linkages with the visitor to a protected area and the local entrepreneur. Political instability can also affect the volume of visitors.

The Koroyanito CBT Development in Fiji: A Case Study

(Summarized and published by The Mountain Institute, 2000, from the Proceedings of the Ecotourism for Forest Conservation and Community Development Conference, 1997).

This example from Fiji has been chosen to highlight the linkages between conservation, economic development and participation in Community-based Tourism products. A key feature in this case was the nature of participation where there appeared to be considerable power held by local communities in the development and management of the tourism product.

As part of the management strategy for Koroyanitu National Park in Fiji the following activities and organizations were established.

Village Ecotourism Co-op Society Limited: Each village with an ecotourism facility established their own Ecotourism Cooperative Society Limited, with the main objective to "establish and manage projects in such a manner, which maximizes benefits to the community and ensures equal opportunities for all". Membership is restricted to landowning units on the basis of the amount of their land included in the project area and villagers who earn their share through direct involvement and/or capital contribution. The first criterion provides an incentive for landowning units to dedicate as much of their land as possible and discourage poor practices, which may disqualify a parcel of land. The second provides for allocation of equity, distribution of benefits, commensurate with one's contribution to the project. The feature to note here is who owns the land that is to be conserved and serves as an attraction. With local ownership, the economic incentives to conserve are much stronger since local people who derive economic benefits also make the decisions on land management.

Koroyanito Development Trust (KDP): All landowning villages agreed to establish the KDP and the objectives were to:

- ensure the protection and integrity of the natural and cultural heritage within the national park
- facilitate efficient and controlled flow of visitors to facilities
- award contracts and approve participation
- and, hold shares in Fijian Vanua Tours Inc.

An institutional arrangement was established to manage conservation and development activities associated with the site.

Fijian Vanua Tours Inc. (FVTI): The objectives of this entity are to:

- promote participation in the protection of their natural and cultural heritage
- secure funding for the establishment of ecotourism facilities and other activities which lend to sustainable development
- conduct relevant training and development programs for owners
- provide management and technical assistance to Village Tourism Cooperatives
- and, hold shares in Fijian Vanua Tours Limited on behalf of accredited facility owners Fijian Vanua Tours Limited

This entity is a limited liability company designed to:

- promote Koroyanitu as a desirable ecotourism destination
- facilitate efficient and controlled flow of visitors to FTVI facilities
- set and enforce standards
- approve accreditation
- generate income

Participation is restricted to two parties - 50% for FVTI and 50% for a private investor who can inject expertise and capital to ensure survival in the tourism industry. Both of the above entities serve to increase participation in tourism and related activities from deriving economic returns to quality control to market and product development.

Noted achievements of the scheme are:

Education: participation in business management and tour guiding courses

Women's participation: active club that makes and sells handicrafts

Environmental protection: logging has not been reintroduced; area set aside for tree nursery; enrichment planting in previously logged areas; etc.

Income: project earned in 1994 the equivalent of the entire communities yearly income before the project, two thirds was retained in the village

Capital additions and improvements: in 1994 another accommodation facility designed especially for school groups who want to camp in the park during field trips. Education groups have regularly used this facility.

The Role of Non-Governmental Organizations in Community Based Tourism

Nongovernmental organizations, or NGOs, are generally accepted to be organizations which have not been established by governments or agreements among governments. In the early 1990s there began to be recognition of the importance of NGOs. They are found to have closer ties to on-the-ground realities in developing countries and, perhaps more important, to be able to deliver development aid considerably more cheaply than states or intergovernmental organizations.

Aided by advances in information and communications technology, NGOs have helped to focus attention on the social and environmental externalities of business activity. Multinational brands have been acutely susceptible to pressure from activists and from NGOs eager to challenge a company's labor, environmental or human rights record. Even those businesses that do not specialize in highly visible branded goods are feeling the pressure, as campaigners develop techniques to target downstream customers and shareholders. In response to such pressures, many businesses are abandoning their narrow shareholder theory of value in favor of a broader, stakeholder approach which not only seeks increased share value, but cares about how this increased value is to be attained. Such a stakeholder approach takes into account the effects of business activity—not just on shareholders, but on customers, employees, communities and other interested groups.

There are many visible manifestations of this shift. One has been the devotion of energy and resources by companies to environmental and social affairs. Companies are taking responsibility for their externalities and reporting on the impact of their activities on a range of stakeholders. Nor are companies merely reporting; many are striving to design new management structures which integrate sustainable development concerns into the decision-making process.

NGOs have been involved with tourism related issues for a long time. Current international activities in community tourism planning and development reflect a strong interest and involvement by NGOs, particularly those focused on resource conservation. Traditionally, they have been critical. They have campaigned against contentious issues, such as tourism links to child prostitution and the forced relocation of peoples for new developments. NGOs have frequently been concerned with tourism related environmental issues, opposing, for example, the establishment of golf courses in developing world locations that have exploited land and water previously available to local communities. NGOs have also focused their attention on the flow of income from tourism, particularly in the developing world, examining how this has been generated and how equitable its distribution is. Most NGOs commenting on tourism have had their major interests elsewhere.

However, NGOs can play an important constructive role in the development of management strategies and in the planning process of tourism development for various reasons. Tourism is becoming far too commoditized, and NGO involvement offers alternative ways of viewing the tourism experience. NGOs have prioritized development approaches that include host community perspectives, emphasized host–visitor interaction and stressed nature and cultural conservation. A number of NGOs have been actively involved in tourism related projects. The motives of NGOs in these circumstances appear to have been to boldly go where government or private commercial organizations would find political or economic resistance. Being nongovernmental institutions they can establish and facilitate the participation of local stakeholders. Being non-profit organizations, they can promote the sustainable use of biodiversity and cultural resources and point out the economic benefits of the integration of tourism development and nature/culture conservation. Being experts in ecological sciences, social development and project management, and having a deep insight into the regional political and economic structures, NGOs can contribute significantly to the sustainability of community based tourism development. NGOs can sensitize the public and even organize mass movements if avaricious industrial interests placate the wider goals of community centered tourism development. Thus, they can act as brokers between conflicting groups and some of them have the potential to act in a conflict management capacity.

Another role that NGOs can take over is that of a co-operative agency that manages a community's initiatives towards CBT. Where international tour operators are unable to contract ground services to in-country operations or do not employ residents of that country, the amount retained in the destination is obviously lower than if this was not the case. Some NGOs appear to have special skills in collaborative partnerships based upon shared aims with local communities, the private sector and other NGOs. The NGO can become a unified marketing front for the small and medium scale tourism enterprises run by the community members. With the help of e-commerce technologies, such a body can bypass the middlemen like travel agents and tour operators and reach the tourist originating markets directly. With tour operators invariably demanding payment in the visitor's country of origin, the benefits to national economies can vary considerably. This has the potential to make the community's tourism offerings more cost-competitive, too. In these situations the development work of NGOs can be directly supported by tourism income flows, active tourist participation in projects, or through direct and indirect donations to their work.

Thus, NGOs are shown often to be both campaigning and proactive bodies, capable of operating in a wide variety of natural, economic and political environments. In sum, NGOs in community based tourism does one or more of the following things:

1. Contribute to the development of policies and plans for the CBT industry
2. Assist the government in developing a standard for responsible community based tourism
3. Assist the government, private sector and communities in implementing, monitoring and evaluating CBT
4. Attract funding from donor agencies to develop specific CBT projects
5. Assist communities and community groups in organizing themselves, preparing themselves for CBT and implementing CBT projects
6. Assist the government in conducting tourism and environmental awareness programs among communities and the tourism industry at large
7. Liaise between the private sector and communities

to generate more community involvement in the tourism sector and stronger private sector commitment

8. Deliver education, training, bridging courses, and other capacity building exercises to local communities
9. Resist against inequitable tourism development by campaigning and mobilizing community support
10. Manage and market the community tourism product for the community, at least until the community gains experience to manage on its own.

Some of NGOs that do outstanding work in the area of tourism are:

- Tourism Concern *(www.tourismconcern.org.uk)*
- Equations in India *(www.equitabletourism.org)*
- Ecumenical Coalition on Third World Tourism *(www.ecotonline.org)*
- World Wide Fund for Nature *(www.wwf.org)*
- Conservation International *(www.conservation.org)*
- Rainforest Alliance *(www.rain-forest-alliance.org)*
- Cultural Restoration Tourism Project *(http://home.earthlink.net/~crtp)*
- International Council on Monuments and Sites *(www.icomos.org)*
- International Society for Eco-tourism Management *(www.ecomanage.com)*
- Partners in Responsible Tourism *(www2.pirt.org)*
- Retour Foundation *(www.retour.net)*

Governments and Community Based Tourism

Community Based Tourism can not be implemented successfully without the constant and coordinated facilitation by the various governmental bodies. Governments play a critical role through their institutional leadership, guaranteeing stakeholders' participation. The Governments' role is also essential in the establishment of regulatory and policy frameworks, ensuring their enforcement, the application of appropriate economic instruments (including the removal of environmentally perverse subsidies), and monitoring environmental quality. What communities do in tourism depends on the opportunities and power they have, the incentives and prices they face, and their access to skills, training, capital and markets. All of these are shaped by government policies, regulation and taxes. Only governments can provide the strategic planning base for CBT which is so clearly needed. Only they can ensure that valuable and fragile habitats are identified, that baseline studies and monitoring are carried out, and that overall infrastructure needs and implications are assessed. And only they can establish emissions standards and citing and design requirements, and ensure that they are enforced.

Governments need to make resources such as national tourist boards accessible to CBT operations, while ensuring that systems of licensing or tourism standards do not act as barriers. Government, especially, the local government, provides the core utilities and infrastructure on which the tourism industry is based. This includes district and city roads, lighting, water and sewerage, public transport systems, signs, airports, and ports. If local government operates attractions such as museums, art galleries, sports stadiums, convention centers, parks, gardens, events, tours, and other amenities, the same become additional motivators for tourists to visit a CBT destination. The government can integrate travel information about the CBT destinations in the country into its Visitor Information Network, too.

Private companies can't be expected to share profits and power with rural communities simply because it's a kind thing to do. But governments can create the conditions under which it is in their interests to work with communities by giving communities market power and giving the private sector more security of investment and incentives for partnership. This can be by means of:

- asking private sector bidders to develop proposals for community partnership, and making this a key criteria in allocating tourism rights. This small change to the planning process can force every new investment to address community tourism issues.
- devolving tenure to communities, to give them market power in forming agreements
- giving communities an equity share in government-private agreements
- helping local residents to start private enterprises.

Policies vary from country to country and over time. It is often the overall approach that is most important in helping community tourism to flourish. Some tips that are suggested from governments in CBT by Africa Resources Trust (ART, 2005) are:

- Create supportive attitudes in government
- Let communities develop tourism over time

- Create opportunities and remove constraints, rather than plan community tourism for them
- Recognize that local people will have multiple livelihood objectives, not just maximizing cash income. Concerns about how land or natural resources are used, or access to training, can be equally important to livelihoods
- Enhance their power in the tourism market
- Ensure tourism sector regulations encourage rather than exclude the informal sector
- Welcome NGO facilitation – it's usually needed

There are two extremes to be avoided: one is to ignore community tourism or pretend it will happen with no support from Government and the industry. The other is for government and the industry to try to do everything and do it now, without allowing time for local people to develop their ideas and skills.

Harnessing Public-Private Partnership for Community Based Tourism

Public-private partnership (PPP or P3) is a variation of privatization in which elements of a service previously run solely by the public sector are provided through a partnership between the government and one or more private sector companies. Unlike a full privatization scheme, in which the new venture is expected to function like any other private business, the government continues to participate in some way.

Important variants of public-private partnerships are (Source: National Council for Public Private Partnerships, USA): Build/Operate/Transfer (BOT) or Build/Transfer/Operate (BTO); Build-Own-Operate (BOO); Buy-Build-

Operate (BBO); Service Contracts (SC); Design-Build (DB); Design-Build-Maintain (DBM); Design-Build-Operate (DBO); Developer Finance: Enhanced Use Leasing (EUL); Lease/Develop/Operate (LDO) or Build/Develop/Operate (BDO); Lease/Purchase; Sale/Leaseback; Tax-Exempt Lease; and Turnkey Arrangement.

Build/Operate/Transfer (BOT) or Build/Transfer/Operate (BTO): The private partner builds a facility to the specifications agreed to by the public agency, operates the facility for a specified time period under a contract or franchise agreement with the agency, and then transfers the facility to the agency at the end of the specified period of time. In most cases, the private partner will also provide some, or all, of the financing for the facility, so the length of the contract or franchise must be sufficient to enable the private partner to realize a reasonable return on its investment through user charges.

At the end of the franchise period, the public partner can assume operating responsibility for the facility, contract the operations to the original franchise holder, or award a new contract or franchise to a new private partner. The BTO model is similar to the BOT model except that the transfer to the public owner takes place at the time that construction is completed, rather than at the end of the franchise period.

Build-Own-Operate (BOO): The contractor constructs and operates a facility without transferring ownership to the public sector. Legal title to the facility remains in the private sector, and there is no obligation for the public sector to purchase the facility or take title. A BOO transaction may qualify for tax-exempt status as a service contract if all Internal Revenue Code requirements are satisfied.

Buy-Build-Operate (BBO): A BBO is a form of asset sale that includes a rehabilitation or expansion of an existing facility. The government sells the asset to the private sector entity, which then makes the improvements necessary to operate the facility in a profitable manner.

Service Contracts: A public partner (federal, state, or local government agency or authority) contracts with a private partner to provide and/or maintain a specific service. Under the private operation and maintenance option, the public partner retains ownership and overall management of the public facility or system. Another way is public partner (federal, state, or local government agency or authority) contracts with a private partner to operate, maintain, and manage a facility or system proving a service. Under this contract option, the public partner retains ownership of the public facility or system, but the private party may invest its own capital in the facility or system. Any private investment is carefully calculated in relation to its contributions to operational efficiencies and savings over the term of the contract. Generally, the longer the contract term, the greater the opportunity for increased private investment because there is more time available in which to recoup any investment and earn a reasonable return. Many local governments use this contractual partnership to provide wastewater treatment services.

Design-Build (DB): A DB is when the private partner provides both design and construction of a project to the public agency. This type of partnership can reduce time, save money, provide stronger guarantees and allocate additional project risk to the private sector. It also reduces conflict by having a single entity responsible to the public owner for the design and construction. The public sector partner owns the assets and has the responsibility for the operation and maintenance.

Design-Build-Maintain (DBM): A DBM is similar to a DB except the maintenance of the facility for some period of time becomes the responsibility of the private sector partner. The benefits are similar to the DB with maintenance risk being allocated to the private sector partner and the guarantee expanded to include maintenance. The public sector partner owns and operates the assets.

Design-Build-Operate (DBO): A single contract is awarded for the design, construction, and operation of a capital improvement. Title to the facility remains with the public sector unless the project is a design/build/operate/transfer or design/build/own/operate project. The DBO method of contracting is contrary to the separated and sequential approach ordinarily used in the United States by both the public and private sectors. This method involves one contract for design with an architect or engineer, followed by a different contract with a builder for project construction, followed by the owner's taking over the project and operating it.

A simple design-build approach creates a single point of responsibility for design and construction and can speed project completion by facilitating the overlap of the design and construction phases of the project. On a public project, the operations phase is normally handled by the public sector under a separate operations and maintenance agreement. Combining all three passes into a DBO approach maintains the continuity of private sector involvement and can facilitate private-sector financing of public projects supported by user fees generated during the operations phase.

Developer Finance: The private party finances the construction or expansion of a public facility in exchange for the right to build residential housing, commercial stores, and/or industrial facilities at the site. The private developer contributes capital and may operate the facility under the oversight of the government. The developer gains the right to use the facility and may receive future income from user fees.

While developers may in rare cases build a facility, more typically they are charged a fee or required to purchase capacity in an existing facility. This payment is used to expand or upgrade the facility. Developer financing arrangements are often called capacity credits, impact fees, or extractions. Developer financing may be voluntary or involuntary depending on the specific local circumstances.

Enhanced Use Leasing (EUL): An EUL is an asset management program in the Department of Veterans Affairs (VA) that can include a variety of different leasing arrangements (e.g. lease/develop/operate, build/develop/operate). EULs enable the VA to long-term lease VA-controlled property to the private sector or other public entities for non-VA uses in return for receiving fair consideration (monetary or in-kind) that enhances VA's mission or programs

Lease/Develop/Operate (LDO) or Build/Develop/Operate (BDO): Under these partnerships arrangements, the private party leases or buys an existing facility from a public agency; invests its own capital to renovate, modernize, and/or expand the facility; and then operates it under a contract with the public agency. A number of different types of municipal transit facilities have been leased and developed under LDO and BDO arrangements.

Lease/Purchase: A lease/purchase is an installment-purchase contract. Under this model, the private sector finances and builds a new facility, which it then leases to a public agency. The public agency makes scheduled lease payments to the private party. The public agency accrues equity in the facility with each payment. At the end of the lease term, the public agency owns the facility or purchases it at the cost of any remaining unpaid balance in the lease.

Under this arrangement, the facility may be operated by either the public agency or the private developer during the term of the lease. Lease/purchase arrangements have been used by the General Services Administration for building federal office buildings and by a number of states to build prisons and other correctional facilities.

Sale/Leaseback: This is a financial arrangement in which the owner of a facility sells it to another entity, and subsequently leases it back from the new owner. Both public and private entities may enter into a sale/leaseback arrangement for a variety of reasons. An innovative application of the sale/leaseback technique is the sale of a public facility to a public or private holding company for the purposes of limiting governmental liability under certain statues. Under this arrangement, the government that sold the facility leases it back and continues to operate it.

Tax-Exempt Lease: A public partner finances capital assets or facilities by borrowing funds from a private investor or financial institution. The private partner generally acquires title to the asset, but then transfers it to the public partner either at the beginning or end of the lease term. The portion of the lease payment used to pay interest on the capital investment is tax exempt under state and federal laws. Tax-exempt leases have been used to finance a wide variety of capital assets, ranging from computers to telecommunication systems and municipal vehicle fleets.

Turnkey Arrangement: A public agency contracts with a private investor/vendor to design and build a complete facility in accordance with specified performance standards and criteria agreed to between the agency and the vendor. The private developer commits to build the facility for a fixed price and absorbs the construction risk of meeting that price commitment. Generally, in a turnkey transaction, the private partners use fast-track construction techniques (such as design-build) and are not bound by traditional public sector procurement regulations. This combination often enables the private partner to complete the facility in significantly less time and for less cost than could be accomplished under traditional construction techniques.

In a turnkey transaction, financing and ownership of the facility can rest with either the public or private partner. For example, the public agency might provide the financing, with the attendant costs and risks. Alternatively, the private party might provide the financing capital, generally in exchange for a long-term contract to operate the facility.

Further details about these variants are beyond the scope of this module. However, learners desirous of knowing the same are advised to consult the website of the National Council for Public Private Partnerships, USA *(http://ncppp.org)*.

There are several basic characteristics of community-based tourism development that make public-private partnerships a possibility (UNESCAP, 2001). First, communities may not have the skills and experience in tourism management. Second, community tourism ventures take time to set up and require a process of intensive capacity building. Third, community tourism ventures may not be profitable when they are initiated.

Partnership is becoming a powerful tool for implementing CBT policies more effectively. PPPs enable the public sector to benefit from commercial dynamism, the ability to raise finances in an environment of budgetary restrictions, innovation and efficiencies, harnessed through the introduction of private sector investors who contribute their own capital, skills and experience. The positive characteristics of PPP arrangements for infrastructure development appear particularly attractive to developing countries like India given the enormous financing requirements, the equally large funding shortfall, the need for efficient public services, availability of a pool of private finance, growing market stability and privatization trends creating a favorable environment for private sector participation (Subramaniam, 2005).

Despite numerous advantages, certain negative aspects - a too large role for governments, partnerships lacking attention to market needs, disproportional investments, inefficiency of public administration, institutionalization of projects and lack of creativity - have to be taken into consideration before going in for any PPP based tourism development since these are antithetical to the spirit of CBT.

According to OECD (1997), good partnership involves a clear definition of roles, competencies, responsibilities and advantages both in public administrations and private enterprises. In particular, the public sector, as an agent of development, may help achieve optimal exploitation of public resources and services, safeguard the environment, and develop human resources. Partnerships must be based on agreements which show the economic benefits for the public/private sector and/or centre/periphery. More and more forms of partnerships are developed in almost all areas of tourism policy. Governments have to play an important role in new ways of organizing this co-operation, notably by defining a clear national strategy for tourism policy which will stimulate and guide innovative partnerships and give incentives to all individual partners to participate in the development.

The Akha Lodge: A Case Study of PPP in CBT

Akha (in Northern Laos) villagers - with their exotic outfits, ancient traditions and traditional way of life - don't usually sit down with urban businesspeople and hammer out business deals. But, that is the scenario set up by GTZ, a German development agency (www.gtz.de) and Exotissimo Travel (www.exotissimo.com). GTZ is working with Akha villagers to set up their own trekking tours in order to offer them an alternative means of income generation. And, Exotissimo has built a reputation as a leader in the travel service industry in South-East Asia. Dedicated offices are situated in Vietnam, Cambodia, Laos, Myanmar and Thailand. In total, we have 14 offices and more than 320 full-time staff.

This Public-Private Partnership coupled with Community-based Tourism (CBT) offers the opportunity for rural communities to access the potential of a global market while helping to minimize any negative impacts tourism development may bring. The model offers an opportunity for the tour company to invest in an authentic village based tour program without having to develop all the skills in community development approaches. The partnership between communities and tour operator is formalized through a contract, in which rights and responsibilities of both business partners are stated. The approach creates local ownership, jobs and sources of income, trains local personnel, and transfers business know-how and technology in a sustainable and participatory manner while at the same time adding an authentic experience to the tour operator's program.

Concluding Remarks

Raising awareness of all stakeholders involved in community-based tourism is essential for promoting an understanding of the beneficial link between conservation and community development. Awareness raising and information dissemination to the community allows for greater self-determination and informed decision-making. Awareness campaign is equally important to other stakeholders involved, as it leads to greater understanding and sensitivity toward the variables involved in implementing community-based tourism.

Conservationists and development professionals have tried to promote community-based tourism since the 1970s. The CBT was a popular intervention during the ecotourism boom of the 1990s. It is now being suggested as a form of pro-poor tourism. However, only a few projects have generated sufficient benefits to either provide incentives for conservation - the objective of ecotourism—or contribute to local poverty reduction.

Community-based tourism is a complex and nascent field of study, and much remains to be learned. Continued information sharing and dissemination of research results are needed to identify better solutions for linking sustainability to the tourism enterprise. Ongoing research is integral to understanding the means by which CBT can be made more economically, environmentally and culturally sustainable. Policy and action should promote continuing research through the provision of financial, academic, technical, and dissemination support.

Bibliography

Books

Tourism Geography

Author: Stephen Wynn Williams

ISBN: 0415142148

Publisher: Routledge

Tourism: Principles, Practices, Philosophies

Authors: Charles R. Goeldner and J. R. Brent Ritchie

ISBN: 0-471-45038-3

Publisher: Wiley

Eco-tourism: An Introduction.

Author: David A Fennell

ISBN: 0415303648

Publisher: Routledge

The Economics of Tourism

Author: M. Thea Sinclair

ISBN: 0415170761

Publisher: Routledge

E-Commerce and Information Technology in Hospitality and Tourism

Author: Zongqing Zhou

ISBN: 0766841405

Publisher: Thomson Delmar Learning

Journals

Annals of Tourism Research

Tourism Geographies

Tourism Management

Journal of Tourism Studies

Journal of Ecotourism

Journal of Sustainable Tourism

Current Issues in Tourism

Tourism Analysis

Websites

www.wikipedia.com (Website of Wikipedia, the free internet encyclopedia)

www.touristplacesinindia.com (Website of Tourist Places in India)

www.unstats.un.org (Website of the United Nations Statistics Division)

www.snh.org.uk (Website of the Scottish Natural Heritage)

www.answers.com (Website of Answers.com)

www.equitabletourism.org (Website of the Bangalore based NGO, EQUATIONS)

www.coolantarctica.com (Website of Cool Antarctica)

www.resourceafrica.org (Website of Africa Resources Trust)

www.tpdco.org (Website of Tourism Product Development Company)

www.unescap.org (Website of UNESCAP)